Oscar Israelowitz's

Guide to
Jewish
New York City

Israelowitz
PUBLISHERS & DISTRIBUTORS
P. O. BOX 228
BROOKLYN, NEW YORK 11229
(718) 951-7072

Library of Congress Catalogue Card Number: 83-80603
International Standard Book Number: 0-9611036-0-4

Printed in the United States of America

Book design by Jane Berger

Cover Photo
Stained Glass Skylight of Brooklyn Jewish Center

Contents

Introduction

WELCOME to New York City, the world's largest Jewish community. There are 1,118,800 Jewish people in New York City, with an additional one million in the surrounding suburbs. The city is composed of five boroughs or counties: Manhattan, Brooklyn, Queens, The Bronx, and Staten Island.

The Jewish community started in 1654 and grew with continuous waves of immigration. The Jewish community paralleled the growth of the city. As public transportation expanded to outlying sections, the Jews soon followed. The nature of Jewish neighborhoods in the city has been one of transience. Once thriving Jewish communities such as Brownsville, the South Bronx, or Harlem are now wastelands and Jewish "ghost towns." Several of the great Jewish institutions, synagogues, and Hebrew schools still stand as monuments and tombstones of these once vibrant Jewish areas. The Jewish communities shifted from one part of the borough to another. Looking at kosher restaurant lists, one can determine where the present Jewish neighborhoods are located.

Getting around the city is fairly simple. All of the boroughs (except Staten Island) are linked by the New York City subway system. Although it is not the prettiest or cleanest looking subway, it is quite efficient and does service the four boroughs of the city twenty-four hours a day. One can ride on any line of the subway for a single token — including free transfers. There are numerous surface (bus) lines in all of the boroughs. A subway token or exact fare is required for a city bus ride. There are several private express bus lines serving all five boroughs as well. There is even a special shuttle bus line linking the two Chassidic communities of Borough Park and Williamsburg, in Brooklyn.

Introduction

This book is designed to help acquaint the visitor with Jewish life in New York City. There are 12 complete walking and driving tours with detailed maps, kosher restaurants, Jewish theaters, museums, landmarks, and synagogues. There's so much to do and see in Jewish New York City, so let's begin.

Manhattan

IN THE BEGINNING...

In the 1650s, Holland was a world power, with colonies in North and South America. One colony, in Recife, Brazil, was part of the Dutch West India Company. In 1654, Portugal conquered Brazil. The new Portuguese regime gave the Jewish inhabitants of Recife the option of either converting to Christianity or leaving. The Jews opted to leave. They set sail for lands offering religious freedom. Some of these wandering Jews landed and settled in the Caribbean islands of Curacao, Jamaica, and Barbados.

One ship fleeing the Recife Expulsion, carrying twenty-three Jewish men, women, and children, wasn't as fortunate in its search for freedom. Their ship, heading for Amsterdam, was captured in the Caribbean Sea by Spanish pirates. A French galleon, the St. Catherine (St. Charles), came to their rescue. The French captain, however, didn't quite understand where these Jews wanted to go. They wanted to go back to Amsterdam, in the "old country," in Holland. He misunderstood and took them to the Dutch colony Nieuw Amsterdam, to the New World, to Manhattan Island.

Their troubles weren't over yet. When the first Jews to arrive in North America got off the French galleon, they were greeted by the anti-Semitic governor of the colony, Peter Stuyvesant. He did not want any Jews living in his colony. Word went back to Amsterdam of this incident. It is important to note that many of the shareholders of the Dutch West India Company were Jewish. Pressure was exerted on Governor Stuyvesant, and he was finally forced to let these Jews in. This was the official beginning of the Jewish settlement in New York City.

7

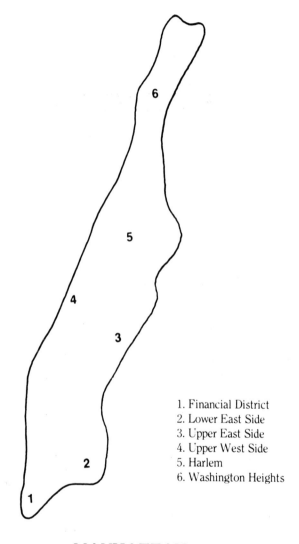

1. Financial District
2. Lower East Side
3. Upper East Side
4. Upper West Side
5. Harlem
6. Washington Heights

MANHATTAN

Walking Tour #1
FINANCIAL DISTRICT

Site of First Jewish Settlement in New York City

How to Get There

By subway, take: IRT Lexington Avenue Express to Bowling Green station; or IRT 7th Avenue Local to South Ferry station; or BMT RR Line to Whitehall Street.

Stop 1. FLAGPOLE   Junction of Whitehall and State Streets

In commemoration of the first Jewish settlement in New York City, the bronze plaque states, "Erected by the State of New York to honor the memory of the twenty-three men, women, and children who landed in September, 1654, and founded the first Jewish community in North America." Notice the Star of David and the Lions of Judah on the upper section of the plaque.

Walk one block along Water Street. Turn left at Broad Street. Walk one block along Broad Street to Fraunces Tavern.

Stop 2. FRAUNCES TAVERN

This is the site of the original Fraunces Tavern where George Washington said farewell to his fellow officers in 1783. The present building is a 1927 reconstruction of the original tavern which stood on this site. The tavern was originally owned by Phila Franks, a descendent of one of the original Jewish settlers of New Amsterdam.

Walk along Broad Street to South William Street. Turn right and walk to No. 26 (Lincoln Square Parking Garage).

Broad Street

Broad Street is one of the widest streets in the Financial District. During the Dutch settlement this street was the site of a man-made canal called the "Heren Gracht," (whose prototype still exists in Amsterdam) which ran from the East River all the way to Wall Street.

9

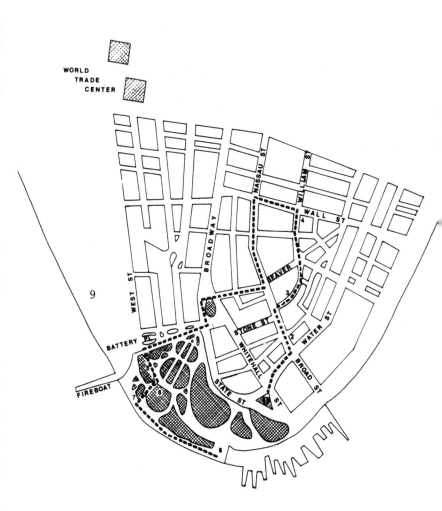

WALKING TOUR #1: FINANCIAL DISTRICT

The canal has been covered-over and incorporated into the New York City sewer system. Some of the streets intersecting Broad Street include Bridge Street, site of a bridge which spanned the canal, and Stone Street, site of the first cobblestone street in New Amsterdam. New Amsterdam became known as New York after the British captured the colony in 1664.

Stop 3. 26 SOUTH WILLIAM STREET

This street, originally called Mill Street, was also known as Jew's Alley — it was the Jewish Ghetto of New Amsterdam. 26 South William Street is the site of North America's first synagogue. The first synagogue in the United States was established by the twenty-three Jews fleeing the Recife, Brazil Expulsion in 1654. They founded the Congregation Shearith Israel (also known as the Spanish and Portuguese Congregation). It was a Sephardic congregation, following the rituals of the Great Spanish and Portuguese Synagogue of Amsterdam. The first synagogue in the country was constructed at this site in 1730. That structure is no longer in existence. In its place is a high-rise parking garage. However, the congregation is still functioning and is located on the Upper West Side of Manhattan at Central Park West and West 70th Street (see TOUR #4). A replica of the Mill Street synagogue is housed in the present structure of the congregation. (NOTE: The Touro Synagogue in Newport, Rhode Island, constructed in 1763, is the oldest existing synagogue structure in the country.)

Continue walking along South William Street for three short blocks, to Wall Street.

Stop 4. WALL STREET

This street was named after the wooden fence which marked the northern boundary of New Amsterdam. It was designed to protect the inhabitants of New Amsterdam against Indian and British attacks from the north. The corner of Wall and South William Streets was the site of Asser Levy's home and slaughterhouse. Asser Levy was one of New Amsterdam's prominent Jewish residents. (A bas relief plaque of the original wall along Wall Street can be seen in the subway station at Broadway and Wall Street — southbound station only. The artwork in the original New York City subway stations was financed by the Jewish banker, August Belmont, in 1904.)

Turn left on Wall Street, walk one block to Nassau Street and turn left. Walk two blocks to Beaver Street and turn right. Walk two blocks

11

to Bowling Green, cross Broadway and walk toward the fireboat sta-
tion. Enter Battery Park at edge of municipal parking lot.

Battery Park

Battery Park is composed of artificial landfill. The base of the high-rise
office buildings on the perimeter of the park marks the area of the original
shoreline of Manhattan island.

Stop 5. THE JERUSALEM GROVE

In honor of the United States' Bicentennial in 1976, the mayor of
Jerusalem, Israel, Teddy Kollek, presented the City of New York with
fifteen Atlas cedars. The stone bearing this historical presentation lies ten
feet behind the park benches. The white stone memorial is composed of
Jerusalem Dolomite (the stone with which all buildings in the city of
Jerusalem are constructed or faced).

Continue walking in Battery Park to an old stone fortress.

Stop 6. CASTLE CLINTON

This fortress was built in 1807 as the West Battery and was designed to
protect New York harbor against possible invasion. The building was later
converted into a concert hall, in which P.T. Barnum introduced Swedish
opera star, Jenny Lind, in 1850. The building later housed the New York
aquarium, before the one in Coney Island was constructed. But between
1855 and 1890 that building was known as Castle Garden, also known, in
Yiddish, as "Kessel Garten." This was the immigrant landing depot, where
over seven million new Americans were processed. It was closed down in
1890 because of political scandals. Castle Garden is today a national
monument.

Walk toward the water's edge, near the fireboat station. Look out into
the harbor.

Liberty Island

Liberty Island is the island on which the Statue of Liberty stands in New
York harbor — a monument and symbol of freedom and hope for millions
of immigrants. The statue was constructed in 1886 and presented by
France to the United States as a gift in honor of its Centennial anniversary.

It was designed by Frederic Bartholdi and engineered by Gustav Eifel. At the base of the statue is a plaque bearing the sonnet "The New Colossus" by the Jewish poetess, Emma Lazarus. The sonnet is recognized by its key phrase, "Give me your tired, your poor, your huddled masses yearning to breathe free." If you cannot get out to Liberty Island, there is a duplicate plaque in Battery Park.

If you are looking out at the harbor, just turn around and look for a raised stone platform, surrounded by hedges (about fifteen feet from the water's edge).

Stop 7. HISTORIC PLAQUE — "THE NEW COLOSSUS"

The historic plaque of Emma Lazarus' sonnet, "The New Colossus," lies flat and imbedded in Jerusalem Dolomite.

Turn around again and look into the harbor. The small island to the right of the Statue of Liberty is Ellis Island. The water towers are still visible atop the main arrivals building.

Ellis Island

Ellis Island, opened in 1892, served as the immigration center after Castle Garden was closed down. Several million immigrants were processed in these facilities. There are fully-escorted tours of the major facilities at Ellis Island. It is part of the Gateway National Park.

It is scheduled to reopen after extensive renovations in 1988.

Walk along the promenade to the ferry terminal building.

Stop 8. FERRIES TO STATUE OF LIBERTY AND ELLIS ISLAND

There are daily ferries to the Statue of Liberty. Ferry service to Ellis Island is daily only from May through October. For further information about ferry schedules, call 269-5755.

Stop 9. HOLOCAUST MEMORIAL & MUSEUM
Battery Park City

The site of the proposed Holocaust Memorial & Museum is located at the southern section of Battery Park City. It will be built as an extension of a luxury housing complex designed by the architectural firm of James Polshek & Associates. It is scheduled to open in the early 1990s.

Walking and Driving Tour #2
LOWER EAST SIDE

How to Get There

By subway, take: IRT Lexington Avenue Lines #4, 5, 6 to Brooklyn Bridge station; or BMT RR Line to City Hall station; or IND A or E train to Chambers Street.

Stop 1. CITY HALL

This is the office of New York City's Jewish Mayor, Edward A. Koch.

Walk seven blocks uptown (north) to White Street and turn left.

Many of the Jewish immigrants who arrived in the 1880s were fleeing the pogroms of Eastern Europe. They arrived unskilled and entered the garment industry, which thrived on low-paying jobs for the unskilled. The sweatshops were housed in the old cast-iron factory buildings in this section known as Tribeca (*tri*angle *be*low *Ca*nal Street). Some of these buildings still house small garment factories while others have been converted into residential loft apartments.

Stop 2. CIVIC CENTER SYNAGOGUE   49 White Street

The Civic Center Synagogue was constructed on the site of a demolished sweatshop. The architects, William N. Breger Associates, designed this synagogue in 1967 as a sculptural abstraction. The building seems to "float in space." There is a cafeteria in the synagogue ballroom which serves hot meals Monday– Thursday from 12 noon– 2 P.M. Mincha services are held upstairs in the synagogue at 12:40 P.M. Monday– Thursday as well. For further information call (212) 966-7141.

Walk back to Broadway and continue onto Bayard Street to Elizabeth Street.

Stop 3. RED BRICK APARTMENT BUILDING
Bayard & Elizabeth Streets

You are now in the heart of Chinatown! One hundred years ago, however, this area was predominantly Jewish. When the architect designed this apartment building his plans included the Star of David that is engraved on the side wall. It was not a religious structure such as a synagogue or

15

WALKING AND DRIVING TOUR #2:
LOWER EAST SIDE

Hebrew school but rather the trademark of the architect.

There are several other tenement structures in the Lower East Side that display similar Judaic decorative treatments.

Continue along Bayard Street to the Bowery and turn right. Walk two blocks then cross Chatham Square. Walk to St. James Place and look for a small park. To the left of that park is a cemetery.

Stop 4. OLDEST JEWISH CEMETERY IN THE UNITED STATES

The remains of the first Jewish settlers of New Amsterdam are buried in this cemetery. This is one of three historic Jewish cemeteries in Manhattan which belong to the Spanish and Portuguese Synagogue, Congregation Shearith Israel. The oldest grave dates back to 1683. The minister of the congregation, Gershom Mendes Seixas, is buried in this cemetery.

The other two cemeteries are located on West 11th Street (east of Avenue of the Americas) and on West 21st Street (west of Avenue of the Americas). Mordecai Manuel Noah, the first political Zionist, who attempted to create a Jewish Agricultural Settlement on Grand Island, New York (near Niagara Falls), in 1825, is buried in the West 21st Street cemetery.

Walk north (uptown) past Chatham square, bear right and continue along East Broadway. Walk two blocks, and under the Manhattan Bridge turn left onto Forsyth Street.

Stop 5. RABBI ISAAC ELCHANAN THEOLOGICAL SEMINARY (*orig.) 47 East Broadway

Named after Rabbi Isaac Elchanan Spektor, a prominent rabbi from Kovno, Lithuania, the Theological Seminary was the forerunner of today's Yeshiva University. It was organized in 1886 at 47 East Broadway and is today located at the main campus of Yeshiva University in Manhattan's Washington Heights.

Walk under Manhattan Bridge, turn left onto Forsyth Street.

Stop 6. CONGREGATION MISHKAN ISRAEL SUWALKI (*orig.) 27 Forsyth Street

Opposite the Manhattan Bridge stand the remains of a former synagogue.

---

* The author uses the abbreviation "orig." to designate that the named institution is no longer functioning.

Walk around the corner (doubleback) to Eldridge Street.

Stop 7. ELDRIDGE STREET SYNAGOGUE   14 Eldridge Street

Built by Eastern European immigrants in 1886, the Eldridge Street Shul, Congregation Kahal Adas Jeshurun Anshei Lubz, is an official New York City and National Historic Landmark. It was the first Orthodox synagogue built specifically as a Jewish house of worship in the Lower East Side. Other major congregations simply purchased former churches and renovated them into synagogues (e.g. Bialystoker Synagogue, Roumanian-American Synagogue, and the Bais Hamedrash Hagadol). The Eldridge Street synagogue was designed by the architectural firm of the Herter Brothers. They were better known as interior decorators for such fashionable clients as the Vanderbilts.

The façade of the building is eclectic; incorporating Romanesque, Gothic, and Moorish elements. The main sanctuary has not been used since the 1930s. It is an immense and opulent room with elaborate brass chandeliers with Victorian glass shades hanging in the midst of a huge, barrel-vaulted space. The Ark was designed in Italian walnut.

Walk north to 58 Eldridge Street. The seven floor tenement building houses J. Levine Co., the complete department store of Judaica.

Exterior view of the landmark Eldridge Street Synagogue, built in 1886.

Walk along Eldridge Street to the corner of Canal Street. Turn left and walk one block to Pike Street. Turn right and continue to East Broadway.

Stop 8. CONGREGATION SONS OF ISRAEL KALVARIE
15 Pike Street

Built in 1903, the Kalvarie Synagogue was the scene of major Jewish ceremonies. The first Rabbi Isaac Elchanan Theological Seminary ordination was held at the Kalvarie Synagogue in 1906. Semicha (ordination) was granted to three rabbis. More recently, the synagogue was the site of the funeral of Rav Aaron Kotler, which was attended by thousands of mourners. In 1917, this congregation had an uptown branch in Harlem. In 1978, several members of the congregation sold the Pike Street building to a Chinese church — without the knowledge or approval of the entire congregation. The case was brought to litigation. After two years in the courts, the sale was nullified. The synagogue today belongs to its Jewish membership. There are no services and there is no caretaker. The doors are boarded up and the once-elegant stained glass windows have all been smashed.

Continue on Pike Street to Henry Street, turn left.

Stop 9. CONGREGATION CHEVRE MISHKAN ANSHEI ZETEL
135 Henry Street

One of the few remaining *shteeblech* in the area. At the turn of the century it is reported that there were several hundred *shteeblech* in the Lower East Side.

Continue walking eastward.

Stop 10. RABBI ISAAC ELCHANAN THEOLOGICAL SEMINARY
(orig.)   156 Henry Street

Initially built to house the Rabbi Isaac Elchanan Theological Seminary in 1904, this building later housed Congregation Agudath Anshei Mamud, and presently houses a Chinese church.

Continue walking along Henry Street.

Stop 11. YESHIVA RABBI JACOB JOSEPH (orig.)
203 Henry Street

In 1899, Rabbi Jacob Joseph from Vilna, Lithuania, was appointed chief rabbi of the Beth Hamedrash Hagadol (60 Norfolk Street). The yeshiva, named in his honor, was built in 1913. It was one of the most prominent yeshivas in the city. It moved from this location in 1976 and relocated to Staten Island. The buildings of the yeshiva at Henry Street now stand abandoned.

Double-back to Pike Street, turn right, walk one block to East Broad-way and turn right.

Stop 12. TENEMENTS 137-139 East Broadway

"Tenement" is the term used to describe a five- or six-story, walk-up, apartment building. Many buildings of this style, designed for the masses of immigrants who came to New York City after the 1870s are located in the Lower East Side. A typical floor plan (a view from a helicopter looking straight down at the building, with the roof removed) shows the central stairwell leading to a public hallway. There are four apartments on each floor. The dumbwaiter and toilets or water closets (WC) are out in the public hallway. There were no showers or baths in these cold-water flats. Once a week, the immigrants would go to the public bathhouse (such as the one on Allen Street). The living room served as a multi-purpose kitchen and dining area. It was common to find ten people sharing one room. To make ends meet, many of the large immigrant families would take in boarders. Each building has indentations on either side to allow air and light to enter each apartment. Looking at the typical floor plan it is easy to see why these buildings were called "dumbbell tenements."

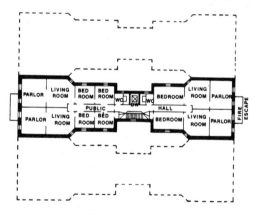

TYPICAL TENEMENT FLOOR PLAN

The Stars of David on the exterior of these tenements are just for decorative treatment. The buildings were never utilized as religious structures, such as a synagogue or Hebrew school.

Stop 13. MESIVTA TEFERETH JERUSALEM
145 East Broadway

Of the many yeshivas and rabbinical academies in the Lower East Side, Mesivta Tifereth Jerusalem (MTJ) is the last survivor. Its Rosh Yeshiva (head Rabbi) is the world-renowned Torah scholar, Rabbi Moshe Feinstein.

Continue walking eastward along East Broadway.

Stop 14. GARDEN CAFETERIA (orig.)   165 East Broadway

This landmark Jewish eatery was the meeting place of Yiddish artists, playwrights, and actors in the 1920s and 1930s. The building was recently sold to a Chinese restaurant (non-kosher). The famous mural on the wall of the Garden Cafeteria, which was supposed to have been removed and placed in the Jewish Museum has seemed to "vanish!" Nobody can account for its disappearance.

Continue walking eastward along East Broadway.

Stop 15. THE JEWISH DAILY FORWARD BUILDING
175 East Broadway

The Jewish Daily Forward (Forverts, in Yiddish) was founded in 1897. Its publisher from 1903 to 1951 was Abraham Cahan. He introduced a special feature called "A Bintel Brief" (a bundle of letters), the Yiddish equivalent to Dear Abby. The Forward Building, one of the largest structures in the Lower East Side, also housed the main headquarters of the Workman's Circle (Arbiter Ring) as well as many other Jewish social and benevolent organizations and burial societies. The Jewish Daily Forward and the Workman's Circle moved to 45 East 33rd Street. The Forward Building now houses a Chinese church. The Yiddish sign (Forverts) in terra cotta still appears on the roof. The building has recently been declared an official New York City landmark.

Cross the street to Seward Park.

Stop 16. SEWARD PARK

This vest-pocket park was created in 1900 by the demolition of two blocks of tenements. It was *the* place where the newly-arrived immigrants would

The Jewish Daily Forward building sign in Yiddish, Forverts.

gather to schmooz. On special occasions such as election returns, the park was jammed with thousands of people who would look at the Forward Building, across the street, at the flashing news sign, in Yiddish.

Continue walking eastward on East Broadway.

Stop 17. EDUCATIONAL ALLIANCE   197 East Broadway

Organized in 1889, the Educational Alliance was the first settlement house in the United States. It was organized by the wealthy "Uptown Jews" — members of the German-Jewish community that had itself made the Lower East Side its original home. The Uptown Jews felt an obligation to help-out the newly-arrived poor Jews downtown, and wanted, at the same time, to prevent anti-Semitism against their coreligionists. They helped "Americanize" these newly-arrived immigrants in this institution. The Educational Alliance building was designed by the Jewish architect, Arnold Brunner, in 1891. Brunner was responsible for the designs of New York City's major synagogues such as the Spanish and Portuguese Synagogue, Temple Shaaray Tefila, and Temple Israel of Harlem. The Educational Alliance assisted in the careers of many notable personalities such as Eddie Cantor, Arthur Murray, Chaim Gross, and Sholom Aleichem. The Educational Alliance today serves the Jewish and Hispanic communities of the Lower East Side.

Continue walking eastward along East Broadway to the junction of Grand Street.

Stop 18. SHTEEBL ROW   225-283 East Broadway

Between 1880 and 1924 more than two million Jews emigrated to New York City. They came with their entire families and, in many instances, with their entire communities. They established over three hundred synagogues in the Lower East Side, some of which occupied the synagogue buildings left behind by previous groups of Jews who moved uptown, but most of which were of the storefront or back-room *(shteebl)* variety, organized according to the country town of origin. The last of these shteeblech are located in this cluster known as "Shteebl Row."

Stop 19. EAST SIDE MIKVEH — RITUALARIUM
313 East Broadway

Built in 1904 as the Arnold Toynbee Hall, this structure served as a settlement house or community center which provided educational and recreational activities for the newly-arrived immigrants in the Lower East Side. The initials "ATH" still appear in the stone balustrade over what had once been the main entrance. The building later housed the Young Men's Benevolent Association and is today the East Side Mikveh. A mikveh or ritual bath, is an important part of life for Orthodox Jewish women, who must attend as part of the preparation for marriage, and who are required to cleanse themselves in it every month. According to the Scriptures, the water must be natural, such as rain or spring water. It is collected in a pool or cistern which measures 40 *s'ah* (an ancient measurement). There are usually other pools of water which are heated surrounding the center pool. A pipe connecting each surrounding pool creates an integration of the waters *(hashakah)* which purifies all the waters in the mikveh. Tours of the mikveh are available by appointment only, 475-8514.

Turn left on Grand Street. Cross the street and walk one block. Turn right on Willett Street.

Stop 20. BIALYSTOKER SYNAGOGUE   7 Willett Street

Built in 1826 as the Willett Street Methodist Church, the fieldstone (Manhattan schist) structure is an official New York City landmark. The Orthodox Congregation Anshei Bialystok, which had been organized on Orchard Street in 1878, bought this building in 1905. It is the oldest structure in the city to house a synagogue.

Walk back to Grand Street and walk westward.

Stop 21. HENRY STREET SETTLEMENT PLAYHOUSE 466 Grand Street

The Henry Street Settlement (located at 265 Henry Street) was founded in 1893 by Lilian D. Wald, pioneer social worker. The agency was originally called the Nurses' Settlement. Lilian Wald was a nurse as well and organized what is still known today as the Visiting Nurses' Service, which has treated thousands of sick people in their homes. The Playhouse was organized in 1915 as an offshoot of the Henry Street Settlement. It started as a theatre for the Settlement's amateur productions but soon became a house for professional theater as well. Graduates of the acting course given there include Gregory Peck, Tammy Grimes, Diane Keaton, Eli Wallach, and Lorne Greene.

Walk along Grand Street to Norfolk Street and turn right.

Stop 22. BETH HAMEDRASH HAGADOL   60 Norfolk Street

Built in 1852 as the Norfolk Street Baptist Church, the Gothic Revival building was purchased in 1885 by the Orthodox congregation that is still housed in it. It is, therefore, the home of the oldest Orthodox congregation in the city continuously housed in a single location. In 1899, Rabbi Jacob Joseph from Vilna was appointed chief rabbi of the congregation. The Yeshiva Rabbi Jacob Joseph (RJJ) was built in 1913 and was located at 203 Henry Street until it closed down in 1976 and moved to Staten Island. The Congregation Beth Hamedrash Hagadol is an official New York City landmark.

Continue along Grand Street and at Essex Street turn right and walk 150 feet. On a retaining wall of the high-rise apartment building, look for a small plaque.

Stop 23. BIRTHPLACE OF B'NAI BRITH

At what used to be Sinsheimer's Cafe, at 60 Essex Street, is an historic plaque marking the site of the birthplace of the Jewish organization, B'nai Brith, on October 13, 1843.

Cross Essex Street and walk south to Canal Street. Turn right at Canal Street and walk two blocks to Orchard Street.

Stop 24. JARMULOWSKY BANK BUILDING
Canal and Orchard Streets

Mr. Sender Jarmulowsky arrived in the Lower East Side in 1870. He started out selling *shmahtes* (pieces of cloth) with a pushcart on Hester Street. He became financially successful and founded a bank for his fellow immigrants in 1873. His bank building was erected in 1895 and was the tallest structure in the Lower East Side. The bank's finances stood on shaky grounds. After the Panic of 1907 and the founder's death, the bank finally collapsed. Thousands of immigrant depositors were ruined with the bank's failure.

Turn right on Orchard Street and continue for one block to Hester Street.

Stop 25. THE "CHAZIR" MARKET   Hester and Orchard Streets

The sweatshops of the Lower East Side were the scenes of teeming activity and continuous transience. A small contractor would obtain raw material and an order for finished goods from one of the large merchants. He would then obtain the workers he needed for the assignment. In a public shape-up that took place each morning at the intersection of Hester and Orchard Streets, masses of workers and contractors gathered to bargain for jobs. This teeming intersection was called the "Chazir-Mark" (pig market, in Yiddish).

Continue northward on Orchard Street.

Stop 26. TENEMENT   47 Orchard Street

The facade of this tenement has the Stars of David in relief. This was the Jewish builder's decorative treatment of his building. It was not a religious structure such as a Hebrew school or synagogue.

Continue along Orchard Street to Delancey Street.

Stop 27. WILLIAMSBURG BRIDGE

The arrival of hundreds of thousands of East European Jews after 1900 and the razing of entire blocks of East Side slums to make way for the Williamsburg Bridge approach along Delancey Street in 1903 caused a great surge of Jewish migration tò Williamsburg, Brooklyn, directly across the river from the Lower East Side. The pedestrian ramp of the bridge became a major promenade linking the Jewish communities of the Lower East Side and Williamsburg. On Rosh Hashana (Jewish New Year), many hundreds of Jews from each side of the river would go to *Tashlich* along the promenade of the Williamsburg Bridge. Under BROOKLYN see directions for a side-trip to Williamsburg.

Turn left on Delancey Street. Walk one block to Allen Street and turn right.

Stop 28. PUBLIC BATHS   133 Allen Street

The Tenement House Reform Bill of April, 1901, prohibited the further construction of the "dumbbell" tenements that predominated on the Lower East Side. According to the new law, every residential building completed after January 1, 1902 had to allow for direct natural lighting of every room and to conform to such minimal health and safety standards as separate toilet facilities for each apartment and safely constructed fire escapes. The immigrants who, unfortunately, had to live in the old law dumbbell tenements would go, once a week, to the public bathhouses such as the one at 133 Allen Street.

Continue along Allen Street and turn right at Rivington Street.

Stop 29. FIRST WARSHAW CONGREGATION (orig.) 58 Rivington Street

In 1903, Congregation Adath Jeshurun of Jassy was constructed. The congregation later moved out and was replaced by the First Warshaw Congregation. That congregation disbanded as well. Several years ago, the building was purchased by an artist and is today used as his studio.

Continue walking along Rivington Street which becomes a pedestrian mall on Sundays.

Stop 30. FIRST ROUMANIAN-AMERICAN CONGREGATION (SHAAREY SHOMAYIM)   89 Rivington Street

Built as a Methodist Church in 1888, the building was purchased by this Orthodox congregation four years later. Some of the world's greatest cantors officiated in this synagogue including Yossele Rosenblatt, Moshe Kousevitzky, Jan Peerce and his brother-in-law, Richard Tucker. The congregation is still functioning.

Walk to the corner of Rivington and Essex Streets.

Stop 31. ESSEX STREET MARKET

For many of the newly-arrived Jewish immigrants, the sweatshops were the only places where these unskilled laborers could find jobs. The working conditions were intolerable, not only because of the overcrowding and filth but also because they had to work twelve to sixteen hours a day, seven days a week, including the Jewish Sabbath. A sign posted in the sweatshops stated quite simply, "If you don't come in on Saturday, don't come in on Sunday!" Many of the Orthodox immigrants decided to go into business for themselves. They rented pushcarts and made their own "office hours." The streets were filled with these pushcarts, selling everything from "shmahtes" (rags) to buttons. Orchard Street was a major artery for these pushcarts, until they were banned in the late 1930s. The pushcart peddlers moved into the Essex Street Market. Today, there are Jewish as well as Hispanic merchants in the Market.

At this junction, the walking tour becomes a driving tour since many of the stops are in predominantly high-crime zones.

Turn left at Essex Street, drive to Stanton Street and turn right. Drive to Norfolk Street and look to the left.

Stop 32. CONGREGATION ANSHE SLONIM   172 Norfolk Street

This Gothic Revival structure was built in 1849 by the Reform Congregation Anshe Chesed. It was designed by architect Alexander Saeltzer and had a seating capacity of 1500. Anshe Chesed, not to be confused with the present-day Ansche Chesed, a Conservative congregation on the Upper West Side, was organized in 1828, sold the building in 1874 to the Orthodox Congregation Oheb Zedek, and eventually merged with Temple Emanu-El. In 1921, the building was purchased by Congregation Anshe Slonim. It occupied the structure until 1975 when its membership began to dwindle because of the changing neighborhood. At that point, the building was abandoned. The city had plans to demolish the structure. In 1986, however, a Spanish sculptor, Angel Orensanz, purchased the former synagogue for $500,000. He has plans to use part of the building as his studio, convert other parts of the space into artists' lofts, and convert the basement into a community center.

The building has recently been declared an official New York City Historic Landmark. The front façade, therefore, cannot be altered. This is the oldest synagogue structure in New York State.

Continue driving eastward along Stanton Street to Clinton Street. Look to the left.

Stop 33. CONGREGATION CHASAM SOPHER   8 Clinton Street

The second oldest synagogue structure in New York City was built in 1853 by the German Reform Congregation Rodeph Sholom. Rodeph Sholom moved uptown in 1891. Its present structure in the Upper West Side, at 7 West 83rd Street was built in 1930. Congregation Chasam Sopher bought the Clinton Street building in 1891 and is still functioning at that location.

Continue along Stanton Street to #180.

Stop 34. CONGREGATION BNAI YAKOV ANSHE BRAZEZAN 180 Stanton Street

This congregation was organized in 1891. The synagogue building was erected in 1913.

Continue driving along Stanton Street to Ridge Street, turn right. Go one block to Rivington Street, turn right and continue to #150.

Stop 35. STREIT'S MATZOH FACTORY   150 Rivington Street

The only matzoh factory in Manhattan is located at the corner of Rivington and Suffolk Streets. Tours of the facilities are no longer available due to insurance laws. Look through the window and see the modern machinery with conveyor belts carrying consolidated sheets of matzoh before they are broken into squares and packed into boxes.

Stop 36. SCHAPIRO'S WINE COMPANY   124 Rivington Street

Founded in 1899, Schapiro's Wine Factory still uses the original oak wine vats in the basement. Free tours of the facilities are conducted on Sundays or by appointment. The tour includes wine-tasting of its kosher wine products.

Continue driving westward along Rivington Street. At Essex Street, turn right. Drive to Houston Street, turn left but stay on the far right side of the street, which becomes East 1st Street.

Stop 37. CONGREGATION MASAS BENJAMIN ANSHEI PODHAJCE   108 East 1st Street

A functioning tenement-style synagogue.

Continue driving along East 1st Street to First Avenue, turn right and go north to East 6th Street, turn right.

Stop 38. COMMUNITY SYNAGOGUE   325 East 6th Street

Built in 1848 for the United German Lutheran Church in the Romanesque Revival motif. The church group went on an outing to the Bear Mountains in the late 1930s but met with disaster. The boat which the church group was sailing on capsized, drowning the entire congregation. In 1940, the Community Synagogue purchased the building and has been functioning at this location until now.

Continue eastward along East 6th Street.

Stop 39. CONGREGATION AYDUS YISROEL ANSHEI MEZRICH 415 East 6th Street

This congregation was organized in 1892 and built its synagogue in 1910.

Stop 40. CENTER OF THE PROSKUROVE ZION CONGREGATION (orig.)   431 East 6th Street

Continue along East 6th Street past Avenue C. This area is known as the "Alphabet Soup" (bound by Avenues A–D and Houston Street– East 14th Street), containing many abandoned buildings, drug addicts, and one of the highest crime rates in the city.

Stop 41. CONGREGATION AHAVATH YESHURUN SHAARE TORAH (orig.)   638 East 6th Street

The adjoining building on the right was the congregation's Hebrew school.

Drive to Avenue D, turn left, go one block and turn left onto East 7th Street.

Stop 42. BAIS HAMEDRASH HAGADOL ANSHEI UNGAREN (orig.)   240 East 7th Street

This congregation was organized in 1883 and built its tenement-style synagogue in 1905.

Continue driving westward along East 7th Street to #206.

Meticulous inspection of Lulavim at the open air market on Essex Street before the holiday of Succos.

Stop 43. CONGREGATION BNAI RAPPAPORT ANSHEI ROMBROVO (orig.)   206 East 7th Street

This congregation was organized in 1885 and built its tenement-style synagogue in 1910. Note the animal reliefs along the cornice of the abandoned structure. They symbolize the phrases from the Hebrew ethical writings, *Pirkei Avos*, "Be bold as a leopard, light as an eagle, swift as a deer, and strong as a lion."

Drive to Avenue B, turn right, go one block to East 8th Street, turn right.

Stop 44. EAST SIDE HEBREW INSTITUTE (orig.)
Corner Avenue B & East 8th Street

At the turn of the century the area north of Houston Street was predominantly Jewish. It had several tenement-style synagogues and its Yeshiva or Hebrew school. The East Side Hebrew Institute moved into this building before World War I. It is no longer a functioning Hebrew school. The building now houses residential apartments. The Hebrew name entablature above the main entrance is still visible. A Star of David is also still present near the top windows of the structure.

Continue along East 8th Street to #317.

Stop 45. FORMER SYNAGOGUE   317 East 8th Street

Continue on East 8th Street to Avenue C, turn right, go one block to East 7th Street and drive to Second Avenue.

Stop 46. SECOND AVENUE — THE JEWISH RIALTO

Second Avenue was widely known as the Jewish Rialto because of its many Yiddish theaters. Among the remaining theater buildings along the Avenue are the Yiddish Art Theatre, once known as the Eden Theatre (now the Enter Media Theatre) at East 12th Street, the Anderson Yiddish Theatre at East 4th Street (now abandoned), and the Orpheum, at St. Marks Place.

Walk westward along East 7th Street.

Stop 47. HEBREW ACTOR'S UNION   31 East 7th Street

Just west of the Jewish Rialto (the Yiddish Theatre District along Second Avenue) is the Hebrew Actor's Union, which is still active.

Walk westward along East 7th Street to Third Avenue. Turn left and walk to East 4th Street. Turn right at East 4th Street and walk westward to Broadway.

Stop 48. HEBREW UNION COLLEGE — JEWISH INSTITUTE OF RELIGION   1 West 4th Street

In 1922, Stephen S. Wise founded the Jewish Institute of Religion in New York to provide training "for the Jewish ministry, research, and community service." Rabbi Wise was its president until 1948. The school was located adjacent to his Free Synagogue at 30 West 68th Street in the Upper West Side until its present building was completed in 1980. The Jewish Institute of Religion merged with the Hebrew Union College (whose main campus is in Cincinnati, Ohio) in 1950. The College prepares its students for the pulpit in congregations belonging to the Reform Movement.

Continue walking westward along West 4th Street for 2 blocks. At Greene Street turn right. Walk along Greene Street to Washington Place.

Stop 49. THE TRIANGLE FIRE   Washington Place & Green Street

A bronze plaque at the northwest corner of Washington Place and Greene Street refers to the site of the Triangle Shirtwaist Company fire, a tragedy which took 146 lives, mostly those of young women, on the Saturday afternoon of March 25, 1911. The Loft Building which stands today on this corner, originally called the Asch Building, is the very building in which the holocaust took place. The Triangle Company occupied the upper three floors of the ten-story structure. The building is now part of New York University campus.

Walking Tour #3
UPPER EAST SIDE

Stop 1. ISAIAH WALL   First Avenue & East 43rd Street (to the right of the Shcharansky Steps)

Opposite the United Nations, on the west side of the street, stands the massive granite monument with the words of the prophet Isaiah inscribed on its face, "They shall beat their swords into plowshares and their spears into pruning hooks. Nation shall not lift up sword against nation, neither shall they learn war any more." The Shcharansky Steps are named in honor of Jewish Soviet dissident, Anatoly Shcharansky.

Walk north to East 47th Street and turn left.

Stop 2. HOLOCAUST MEMORIAL
East 47th Street & First Avenue

On the south side of Dag Hammarskjold Park are the sculptural memorials in honor of the six million Jewish men, women, and children who perished in World War II. The park is the scene of the annual rally for the struggle to save Soviet Jewry, which is held in the spring and is attended by thousands of people. The six bronze plaques were designed by A. Blatas in 1982. International travelers might recognize this monument. There is a similar Holocaust Memorial in the large piazza in the Ghetto of Venice, Italy, which was designed by A. Blatas.

Continue westward on East 47th Street to Lexington Avenue, turn right and walk to East 55th Street.

Stop 3. CENTRAL SYNAGOGUE
Lexington Avenue & East 55th Street

Organized by Bohemian Jews in 1839, Congregation Shaaray Hashamayim merged with Congregation Ahavat Chesed to create the Central Synagogue. The first buildings of the congregation were located in the Lower East Side. In 1872, the present structure was built. It was designed by the first Jewish architect in America, Henry Fernbach. The design is Moorish Revival and is an exact copy of the largest synagogue in Europe,

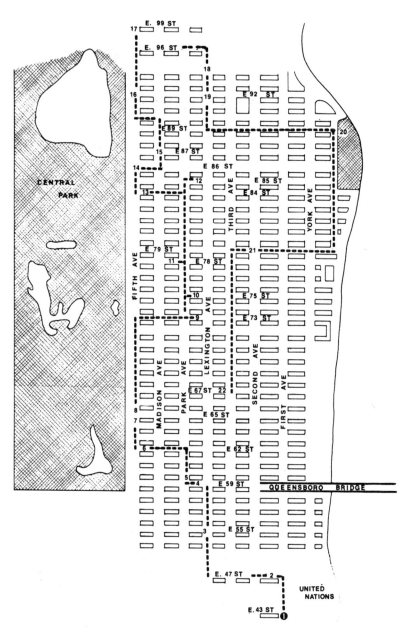

WALKING TOUR #3: UPPER EAST SIDE

the Dohany Ucta Synagogue, in Budapest, Hungary. The Budapest Temple was constructed in 1859 and has a seating capacity of 3300. The Central Synagogue has a seating capacity of over 1300. The cornerstone of the Central Synagogue was laid in 1870 by Rabbi Isaac Mayer Wise, whose son later became rabbi of the congregation. The Central Synagogue follows the Reform ritual. It is an official New York City, New York State, and national historic landmark. It is the oldest synagogue building in continuous use by one congregation in New York City. Tours are available by appointment only. Call 838-5122.

Walk uptown (north) along Lexington Avenue. Turn left at East 59th Street. Walk one block to Park Avenue.

Exterior view of the landmark Central Synagogue, built in 1872.

Guide to Jewish New York City

Stop 4. FEDERATION OF JEWISH PHILANTHROPIES
130 East 59th Street

Occupying five floors of this high-rise office building, the Federation provides philanthropic support to 130 affiliated institutions.

Stop 5. THE JEWISH AGENCY   515 Park Avenue

The New York City headquarters of the Jewish Agency. Extremely tight security measures are taken before one can enter the offices of the Aliyah and Ulpan Centers, the American Zionist Federation, or the American Zionist Youth Foundation.

Walk uptown along Park Avenue. Turn left at East 62nd Street.

Stop 6. FIFTH AVENUE SYNAGOGUE   5 East 62nd Street

Percival Goodman designed over fifty synagogues throughout the United States. His only synagogue in Manhattan, the Fifth Avenue Synagogue, occupies the site of a typical townhouse of the Upper East Side. The facade contains sharply incised oval-pointed windows which are filled with stained glass. Built in 1959, this synagogue reflects a sculptural and expressionistic design.

Walk to Fifth Avenue, turn right and walk to East 65th Street.

Stop 7. HOUSE OF LIVING JUDAISM
838 Fifth Avenue

Headquarters of the Reform Movement in the United States, the Union of American Hebrew Congregations, the National Federations of Temple Brotherhoods, Sisterhoods, and Youth, and the New York Federation of Reform Synagogues, the North American section of the World Union for Progressive Judaism, the National Association of Temple Administrations, and the American Conference of Cantors are all housed in this building. Judaic exhibits are on display on the ground floor of the House of Living Judaism.

Stop 8. TEMPLE EMANU-EL   1 East 65th Street

Organized in 1845, Temple Emanu-El is New York's first Reform congregation. Its first location was in the Lower East Side. In 1868, Temple Emanu-El built its lavish twin-tower Moorish Revival synagogue on Fifth Avenue and East 43rd Street. It was designed by the architectural firm of Leopold Eidlitz and Henry Fernbach. The New York Times described the structure as the "architectural sensation of the city." This building's design inspired other Reform congregations to design their new temples in a similar motif. Some of these structures include: The Barnert Memorial Temple in Paterson, New Jersey (built in 1892 but demolished in the 1950s); Temple Emanu-El in Kingston, New York (built in 1892 but now used as a church); Emanu-El Congregation in Willemstad, Curaçao (built in 1867 but now used as a social hall). Temple Emanu-El's Fifth Avenue and 43rd Street structure was demolished in the 1920s.

In 1929, Temple Emanu-El built the world's largest Reform temple in the world. It is located on the corner of Fifth Avenue and East 65th Street, on the site of the old Vincent Astor mansion. The temple's vestibule walls and floors are Siena travertine; the ceiling is walnut. The walls of the building are actually bearing or self supporting. The main body of the auditorium is 77 feet wide, 150 feet in length, and 103 high. The seating capacity is 2,500.

The Sanctuary (Ark area) is 30 feet in depth and just over 40 feet wide, with a marble floor and marble (and mosaic) wainscot on the sides. Below the massive arch is the Ark, with columns of French Benou Jaume marble. The Ark doors are bronze, and the frame of the opening is of Siena marble with mosaic insets. The columns are crowned with small bronze tabernacles.

Twenty five feet above the Sanctuary is the choir loft, cut off by a pierced railing surmounted by marble columns of varied colors. The great organ, located above the chancel, is four manual, having 116 speaking stops, 50 couplers, 7,681 speaking pipes, 32 bell chimes, and 61 celestia bars.

The rose window, Gothic in design, is located above the main entrance on Fifth Avenue. The stained glass was designed in England. The twelve petals are symbolic of the twelve tribes of Israel. There are four stained glass windows in the main auditorium which depict historic synagogues. The former temple building, at Fifth Avenue and East 43rd Street and Temple Beth El, which merged with Temple Emanu-El in 1927 and was located on Fifth Avenue and East 76th Street, are portrayed at the southwest corner window (at eye level). The Alt-Nue Shul in Prague, Czechoslovakia and the Rashi Shul in Worms, West Germany are portrayed in stained glass at the northeast corner windows (about 15 feet above the floor).

The Beth El Chapel adjoins the main auditorium of Temple Emanu-El. It is named for Temple Beth El which merged with Emanu-El in 1927. This exquisite chapel is designed in the Byzantine motif. It is used for small weddings, and Bar and Bat Mitzvahs. The two domes of the chapel are supported by six columns of pink Westerly granite, while the side walls rest on arches springing from columns of Breche Oriental marble. Verdello marble is used for the wainscots.

The Sanctuary arch, in which blue is the dominant color, has a golden brown mosaic background with the Ten Commandments inscribed in blue, against which the Ark of wrought steel is set. The stained glass windows above the Ark, depicting the Holy Land, was designed by Louis Comfort Tiffany.

For information about services and tours of Temple Emanu-El, please call (212) 744-1400.

Stop 9. LEO BAECK INSTITUTE   129 East 73rd Street

The Leo Baeck Institute specializes in material about Jewish life and history in Germany and other German-speaking areas in Europe. There are extensive collections of historic documents, books, manuscripts, and photographs. The second-floor gallery is reserved for special exhibitions.

Walk back to Park Avenue, turn right and continue uptown to East 75th Street. Turn left onto East 75th Street.

Stop 10. TEMPLE ISRAEL OF NEW YORK   112 East 75th Street

Organized as the Orthodox Congregation Hand in Hand, in Harlem in
1873, the congregation adopted the reform ritual in 1888 and changed its
name to Temple Israel. Its second home, located at Lenox Avenue and
West 120th Street, was designed by the Jewish architect, Arnold Brunner,
in 1907. The congregation moved to 210 West 91st Street in the Upper
West Side during the 1920s and finally to its present home at 112 East
75th Street.

*Walk back to Park Avenue and continue uptown to East 78th Street.
Turn left onto East 78th Street.*

Stop 11. RABBI JOSEPH H. LOOKSTEIN UPPER SCHOOL
OF RAMAZ   60 East 78th Street

The Ramaz School, a private Jewish Day School, is modern and progressive
in its approach. Religious and secular studies are alternated and, when
possible, are correlated and integrated. The architects of the Upper School,
Conklin and Rossant, have designed a baffling facade. The angle windows
on the upper level of the front facade appear as a painter's garret and are
actually used as the school's art studio. The arched forms (windows and
pinnacles) appear as bay windows or can be interpreted to read as the
domes of Jerusalem or the Tablets of the Law (Ten Commandments).

Walk uptown along Park Avenue. Turn right at East 85th Street.

Stop 12. CONGREGATION KEHILATH JESHURUN
125 East 85th Street

This congregation is the sponsor of the Ramaz School. Ramaz is named
after Rabbi Moses Zevulun Margolies, the Rabbi of the congregation for
thirty-one years. The 1902 synagogue was designed by George Pelham. It
was modeled after the West End Synagogue of Shaaray Tefila at 166 West
82nd Street, on the Upper West Side. That building was designed in 1894
by the Jewish architect, Arnold Brunner. The Pike Street Shul, Congregation Sons of Israel Kalvarie (in the Lower East Side), built in 1903, looks
like a duplicate of Kehilath Jeshurun. The front stoop of Kehilath Jeshurun
was removed in 1948.

Walk west to East 84th Street

41

Stop 13. AMERICAN JEWISH CONGRESS   15 East 84th Street

The former mansion of Ogden Reid is the headquarters of the American Jewish Congress. The Martin Steinberg Cultural Center is in the back wing of the mansion. It is designed as a gathering place for young Jewish artists, writers, musicians, photographers, and films.

Walk north along Fifth Avenue to East 86th Street.

Stop 14. YIVO INSTITUTE FOR JEWISH RESEARCH
1048 Fifth Avenue

Recognized as the world center for Yiddish research, Yivo has the most complete record of Jewish life in Eastern Europe. Founded in Vilna in 1925, Yivo was moved to New York in 1940 to escape the ravages of the Nazis. There are exhibits based on Jewish themes on the first- and second-floor galleries.

Walk one block eastward to Park Avenue. Turn left and walk one block north to East 87th Street.

Stop 15. PARK AVENUE SYNAGOGUE   50 East 87th Street

Founded in 1882 by a group of German and Hungarian Jews, this congregation developed out of the joining of Congregation Agudath Yeshurim, an Orthodox synagogue on East 86th Street, a Reform temple on East 82nd Street, and Congregation Bikur Cholim on Lexington Avenue and East 72nd Street. The Park Avenue Synagogue is now a Conservative congregation and has recently celebrated its 100-year anniversary. Its rabbi, Judah Nadich, was General Eisenhower's adviser on Jewish affairs in Germany. The eminent artist, Adolph Gottlieb, designed the stained glass windows in the adjoining Milton Steinberg House, which serves as the congregation's educational center.

The magnificent sculpture above the main entrance to the educational center was designed by the famous Israeli sculptor, Nathan Rapoport.

Walk north to East 90th Street, then turn left. Continue to Fifth Avenue and turn right. Walk to East 92nd Street.

Stop 16. THE JEWISH MUSEUM
Fifth Avenue & East 92nd Street

Under the auspices of the Jewish Theological Seminary of America, the Jewish Museum has become the repository of the largest and most comprehensive collection of Jewish ceremonial objects in the world. The museum's notable items include: panels of the famous frescoes of Dura Europos, Syria; mosaics from ancient synagogues in Israel; several Torah arks and Torah ark curtains; and a variety of Torah crowns, breastplates, and pointers. NOTE: This museum is open to the public on Monday-Thursday, 12-5 P.M. and Sunday, 11-6 P.M.

Walk north along Fifth Avenue (also called Museum Avenue because of the multitude of museums situated along this fashionable avenue).

Stop 17. MOUNT SINAI HOSPITAL
Fifth Avenue & East 99th Street

Originally known as "Jews Hospital," it became non-sectarian following the Civil War, in 1866, when it changed its name to Mount Sinai Hospital.

Double-back along Fifth Avenue and turn left at East 95th Street. Continue walking east to Lexington Avenue, turn right.

Stop 18. CONGREGATION ORACH CHAIM
1459 Lexington Avenue

This congregation was organized one hundred years ago and is still serving the Upper East Side/Yorkville community. Many of the congregants are doctors, interns and medical students at Mount Sinai Hospital.

Continue walking southward along Lexington Avenue to East 92nd Street.

Stop 19. 92nd STREET YM & YWHA
Lexington Avenue & East 92nd Street

This is the largest and oldest Jewish Community Center in continuous existence in America. It is the only YMHA in the country that has dormitory facilities. With its varied program of activities in music, dance, drama, and the arts, the 92nd Street Y is an important cultural center for all New Yorkers.

Walk south along Lexington Avenue to East 89th Street. Turn left and continue walking eastward on East 89th Street to East End Avenue.

Stop 20. GRACIE MANSION   East End Avenue & East 89th Street

This is the official residence of the presiding mayor of the City and is currently the home of New York City's Jewish mayor, Ed Koch. Tours of the residence are available by special appointment only.

Walk south along East End Avenue to East 79th Street. Turn right and walk three blocks westward to Second Avenue.

Stop 21. CONGREGATION SHAARAY TEFILA
250 East 79th Street

Breaking away from New York City's first Ashkenaz (German versus Sephardic) congregation, B'nai Jeshurun in 1845, Shaaray Tefila started as an Orthodox congregation in the Lower East Side. The congregation's third structure at 166 West 82nd Street was designed by the Jewish architect, Arnold Brunner, in 1894. It was then known as the West End Synagogue. The congregation officially joined the Union of American Hebrew Congregations (Reform Movement) in 1895. The declining neighborhood in the 1950s witnessed the sale of their West 82nd Street building to the Ukrainian Orthodox Autocephalic Church. The present structure of Shaaray Tefila, at 250 East 79th Street, was originally the Trans-Lux Theatre which was renovated to meet the needs of the congregation.

Walk westward along East 79th Street. Turn left at Third Avenue and walk downtown to East 67th Street. Turn right at East 67th St.

Stop 22. CONGREGATION ZICHRON EPHRAIM (PARK EAST SYNAGOGUE)   163 East 67th Street

Organized in 1888, its 1890 Moorish Revival building was designed by Schneider and Herter. (The Herter Brothers designed the Eldridge Street Synagogue in 1886.) This synagogue was founded by Jews from south Germany as an Orthodox congregation. It is one of the few synagogues still owned by the same congregation which built it. It is an official New York City landmark. It is located directly across the street from the Russian Mission to the United Nations and is the scene of many anti-Soviet rallies.

Walking Tour #4
UPPER WEST SIDE

How To Get There

By subway, take: IRT 7th Avenue Line #1 Local to 86th Street station; or IND AA (CC or B Line during rush hours) to 86th Street station.

Stop 1. THE JEWISH CENTER   131 West 86th Street

The first Jewish Center in the United States was designed by Louis Allen Abramson in 1919. Rabbi Mordecai Kaplan created the Center as a deterrent to assimilation and intermarriage with gentiles by second-generation American Jews by providing the community with a Jewish context for social gatherings. It sponsored youth groups, social clubs and athletic events for young adults. Although the Jewish Center was influential in the development of the Conservative Movement in the United States, it follows the Orthodox ritual.

Yeshiva College classes were first begun at the Jewish Center on September 25, 1928 with 35 students, before its move to the Washington Heights campus. Rabbi Dr. Norman Lamm was the spiritual leader of the Jewish Center for many years. In 1976, he was elected president of Yeshiva University.

Walk westward to Broadway. Turn right and walk uptown along Broadway to West 88th Street. Turn left on West 88th Street.

Stop 2. CONGREGATION B'NAI JESHURUN
257 West 88th Street

This is New York City's first Ashkenazic congregation. It was established in 1825 as an offshoot from the only (Sephardic) synagogue in the city, Congregation Shearith Israel (The Spanish and Portuguese Synagogue), which was organized in 1654. B'nai Jeshurun bought, as its first synagogue building, the First Coloured Presbyterian Church at 112 Elm Street (now called Lafayette Street) in 1825. Its present structure at 257 West 88th Street is the congregation's fifth building. It was designed by Herts and Schneider in 1918 in the Moorish Revival motif.

Walk westward to West End Avenue, turn right and walk one block to West 89th Street. Turn left and walk to Riverside Drive.

45

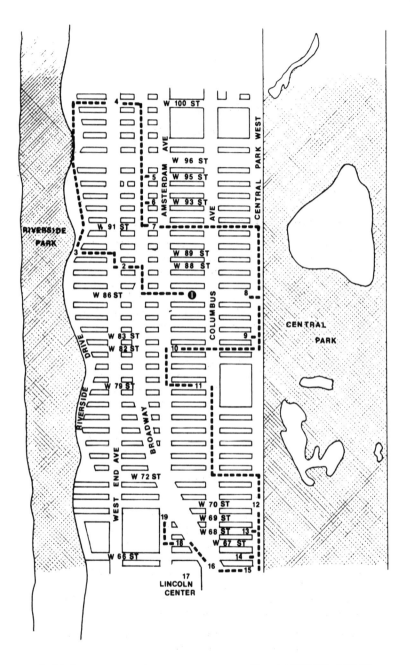

WALKING TOUR #4: UPPER WEST SIDE

Stop 3. YESHIVA CHOFETZ CHAIM   346 West 89th Street

Originally the Issac L. Rice mansion, the building was designed by Herts
and Tallant in 1901. The site is involved in a very bitter controversy. The
Yeshiva received an offer by an anonymous benefactor to replace its
cramped quarters with a new high-rise structure which would incorporate
the Yeshiva in its lower levels and would incorporate cooperative residential apartments above. The concept seemed perfect. However, the existing
high-rise apartment buildings surrounding the present low-rise Yeshiva
would have to sacrifice their unobstructed views of the Hudson River and
the New Jersey Palisades. The case was brought before several judicial
hearings. The decision to turn the Yeshiva building into an official New
York City landmark froze all development plans.

*Walk north along Riverside Drive to West 100th Street. Turn right
and walk one block to West End Avenue.*

Stop 4. TEMPLE ANSCHE CHESED
West End Avenue & West 100th Street

Organized in 1876, Temple Ansche Chesed's present building was designed by Edward I. Shire in 1927. The congregation's previous home was
located in Harlem, at 1881 Seventh Avenue. It was built by the same
architect in 1908. Temple Ansche Chesed follows the Conservative ritual.

The community house, adjoining the temple, houses four separate *min-
yanim.* Each *minyan* follows the Havurah-style of worship where all worshippers, both male and female, have an equal share in the Sabbath service.
It is quite common to find women wearing prayer shawls, leading the service as cantors, and being called up to the Torah for an *aliyah* (recitation of
benedictions for the Torah).

*Walk eastward along West 100th Street to Broadway. Turn right and
walk downtown to West 95th Street. Turn left at West 95th Street.*

Stop 5. CONGREGATION OHAB ZEDEK   118 West 95th Street

The first home of the First Hungarian Congregation Ohab Zedek, which
had been founded in 1873, was at 172 Norfolk Street (in the Lower East
Side) in the synagogue that had formerly belonged to Congregation Anshe
Chesed (Reform). In 1908, after many of its members had migrated uptown
to then-fashionable Harlem, Ohab Zedek purchased its branch at 18 West
116th Street. The world famous cantor, Yossele Rosenblatt, was engaged

in 1912. He officiated in the Harlem synagogue for many years. In the 1920s, the congregation moved to its present location at 118 West 95th Street.

Walk back to Broadway. Continue walking downtown to West 93rd Street. Turn left at West 93rd Street.

Stop 6. CONGREGATION SHAARE ZEDEK
210 West 93rd Street

Originating in the Lower East Side in 1837, this congregation moved to Harlem in 1900. Designed by Michael Bernstein, Congregation Shaare Zedek of Harlem, was one of the prestigious synagogues in the city. It moved to its present site in 1922.

Return to Broadway, continue downtown to West 91st Street. Turn left at West 91st Street.

Stop 7. YOUNG ISRAEL OF THE WEST SIDE
210 West 91st Street

Built for Temple Israel of Harlem in the 1920s, this structure served that Reform congregation until its move to the Upper East Side, at 112 East 75th Street, in 1966. The Young Israel of the West Side is an Orthodox congregation.

Continue eastward to Central Park West. Turn right and walk downtown to West 83rd Street. Turn right at West 83rd Street.

Stop 8. SOCIETY FOR THE ADVANCEMENT OF JUDAISM
(RECONSTRUCTIONIST)   15 West 86th Street

Founded in 1922 by Dr. Mordecai M. Kaplan, the Society, which is the cornerstone of the Reconstructionist Movement, conducts a synagogue and school. Women have complete equality with the men during the synagogue services. They are counted as part of the ten people of a minyan, wear prayer shawls, and are called up to the Torah for *aliyot.* Dr. Kaplan died in November, 1983, at the remarkable age of 102.

Double-back to Central Park West and continue walking south. At West 83rd Street turn right.

Lighting of world's largest menorah during the holiday of Chanukah.

Stop 9. CONGREGATION RODEPH SHOLOM   7 West 83rd Street

This Reform congregation was organized in the Lower East Side in 1842. Its first building, at 8 Clinton Street, erected in 1853, is the second oldest synagogue structure in the city. Its original building is presently used by Chasam Sopher, an Orthodox congregation. Rodeph Sholom's present structure was designed by Charles B. Meyers in 1930. One of its ministers, Rabbi Aaron Wise, who served from 1875-1897, was the father of Rabbi Stephen S. Wise.

Return to Central Park West. Walk one block southward (downtown) and turn right at West 82nd Street.

Stop 10. WEST END SYNAGOGUE (*orig.)   166 West 82nd Street

This structure was originally designed by the Jewish architect, Arnold Brunner, in 1894, for the West End Synagogue-Shaaray Tefila. It served as the prototype design for two other synagogues in the city, Congregation

---

*The author uses the abbreviation "orig." to designate that the named institution is no longer functioning.

Kehilath Jeshurun (125 East 85th Street), built in 1902, and Congregation Sons of Israel Kalvarie (15 Pike Street), built in 1903. The West End Synagogue was sold to a Ukrainian Church in the 1950s. The present home of Temple Shaaray Tefila is located in the renovated Trans-Lux Theatre, located at 250 East 79th Street.

Continue westward to Broadway. Turn left and walk downtown to West 79th Street. Turn left at West 79th Street.

Stop 11. MOUNT NEBO CONGREGATION (orig.)
130 West 79th Street

This Byzantine Revival structure is involved in a bitter controversy. The battle is similar to the one encountered at the Chofetz Chaim Yeshiva (Stop 3.), at 346 West 89th Street. The Mount Nebo Congregation sold its building to a Korean Church several years ago. The building was neglected and even the church could no longer afford the maintenance expenditures. The building is presently abandoned. The roof has rotted through, and rain and snow fall into the main sanctuary. The battle involves local historians,

Exterior view of the Mount Nebo Congregation.

who wish to preserve the building as an endangered sample of Byzantine Revival architecture, and apartment residents, whose windows now yield unobstructed views of Central Park, in opposition to developers of a planned high-rise luxury apartment building which would replace the old, dilapidated synagogue structure.

In July, 1985, the building was demolished. In its place stands a new high-rise condominium.

Walk downtown along Columbus Avenue to West 70th Street, turn left .

Stop 12. THE SPANISH AND PORTUGUESE SYNAGOGUE (CONGREGATION SHEARITH ISRAEL) 99 Central Park West

The oldest Jewish congregation in North America, Shearith Israel, was organized in the Dutch settlement of New Amsterdam in 1654. The first structure built expressly as a synagogue for the congregation was erected in 1730 on Mill Street (now South William Street, in the Wall Street area). The synagogue was enlarged on the same site in 1818. The congregation moved uptown as the neighborhood became an industrial and commercial zone. It moved to Crosby Street, between Broome and Spring Streets (in the Soho District) in 1834. In 1860, the congregation moved to 5 West 19th Street and moved once again to its present location at Central Park West and West 70th Street, in the Upper West Side. The present building was designed in 1897 by the Jewish architect Arnold Brunner in the Classical Revival style.

Although all of the former synagogue buildings are no longer extant, the original furnishings and religious ornaments, including the reading table *(Tebah)*, Holy Ark *(Heychal)*, and even the floorboards have been removed and incorporated into the present building. This adheres to the Rabbinical law which stipulates that the sanctity *(kedushah)* of a synagogue remains in that structure forever. The congregation actually dismantled all of its prior structures in fear that they might be sold to or be used by churches.

The little Synagogue, used for daily services, is a replica of the original Mill Street building. Among the many Torah scrolls that are kept in the Ark, three have been rescued from destruction by the Nazis coming from the Sephardic congregation in the Hague,

51

Netherlands. A pair of silver bells crowning the scrolls bears the name of Myer Myers (1723-1795), a notable New York silversmith in his day. The four silver candlesticks represent an *Havdalah* set, consisting of a candleholder, wine goblet, and spice box—designed to lift apart during the *Havdalah* ceremony (marking the conclusion of the Sabbath day). Made of Spanish brass, the candlesticks may date from the Spanish Inquisition of the 15th century. The *Marranos* or secret Jews had to camouflage their religious practices for fear of being killed. These candlesticks were designed to appear as simple sources of light, but to the secret Jews of Spain they were actually used for their religious service.

The Eternal Light *(Ner Tamid)* has been in continuous use since 1818. Some of the benches (bancas) are from the Mill Street and Crosby Street synagogue buildings. The stained glass windows in both the Little Synagogue and the main sanctuary were designed by Louis Comfort Tiffany.

The reading platform *(Tebah)* in the main sanctuary was intended to be finished in marble, similar to the Holy Ark. The congregation ran out of sufficient funds after it completed the building. A ship's carpenter was commissioned and designed the reading platform in wood, using the shape of the stern of a boat as its model. The congregation was very pleased with the "temporary" design of the reading platform and decided not to replace it with marble.

There are twelve (gas-lit) candlesticks surrounding the reading platform, symbolic of the twelve tribes of Israel. The original Mill Street Synagogue floorboards have been incorporated into the floor of this reading platform. When a member of the congregation is called to the Torah he literally stands on the same floorboards that his Sephardic ancestors stood upon.

Congregation Shearith Israel, also known as the Spanish and Portuguese Synagogue, is an official New York City Historic Landmark. The congregation follows the Western Sephardic (Orthodox) ritual. For information about services and tours of the facilities, please call (212) 873-0300.

Walk downtown along Central Park West to West 68th Street and turn right.

Stop 13. THE STEPHEN WISE FREE SYNAGOGUE
30 West 68th Street

Founded in 1907 by Rabbi Stephen S. Wise, the synagogue uses the word "free" because its pulpit is free, that is, not subject to control. Beginning with Rosh Hashana Eve on October 3, 1910, services were held at Carnegie Hall, giving the Free Synagogue the largest seating capacity of any Jewish congregation in the country. In 1922 the synagogue was housed in the Jewish Institute of Religion (at 40 West 68th Street). That structure was designed by Eisendrath and Horowitz. They incorporated the natural stone indigenous to Manhattan Island (Manhattan schist) for their design—it was as if the synagogue evolved and emerged from the ground as one homogonous entity. In 1949 the Stephen Wise Free Synagogue dedicated its own

building at 30 West 68th Street. It was designed by the firm of Block and Hesse. The Hebrew Union College-Jewish Institute of Religion moved to 1 West 4th Street in 1980.

Continue downtown to West 66th Street and look right.

Stop 14. CONGREGATION HABONIM   44 West 66th Street

On November 9, 1938, Hitler ordered all of the synagogues of Germany destroyed. That was the "Kristalnacht" and marked the beginning of the destruction of the Jewish communities throughout Europe. Congregation Habonim was founded in 1939 by a group of refugees from Nazi Germany. Fragments of the largest temples in Germany (the Essen Temple and the Fassanenstrasse Temple of Berlin) are on display in the lobby of the synagogue.

Continue walking along Central Park West to West 65th Street, turn right.

Stop 15. JEWISH GUILD FOR THE BLIND   15 West 65th Street

The Guild helps blind and visually handicapped people, regardless of race, religion, age, or economic status, to participate in the community on a self-supporting basis.

Walk west along West 65th Street to Columbus Avenue and turn right.

Stop 16. RICHARD TUCKER PARK
Junction of Broadway, Columbus Avenue and West 66th Street

The small island park in the middle of this busy intersection is located opposite Lincoln Center for the Performing Arts. Richard Tucker worked his way up from being a peddler and cantor in the Lower East Side, to the status of being one of the world's greatest operatic tenors. He was known as the "Sweet singer of Israel." He died of a heart attack in 1975. His funeral was held in the Metropolitan Opera House at Lincoln Center.

Cross the interstection and proceed into the plaza of Lincoln Center for the Performing Arts.

Stop 17. CHAGALL PAINTINGS
Metropolitan Opera House, Broadway & East 65th Street

In the lobby of the Metropolitan Opera House are two magnificent paintings by the Jewish artist, Marc Chagall. The 30 ft. x 36 ft. paintings are titled, "The Triumph of Music" and "The Sources of Music."

Walk up Broadway to West 67th Street, turn left.

Stop 18. THE HEBREW ARTS SCHOOL   129 West 67th Street

Founded in 1952, The Hebrew Arts School is a nonprofit, nonsectarian institution dedicated to high-quality instruction in music, dance, art, and theater for children and adults. While she welcomes all comers, Tzipora Jochsberger, the school's founder, emphasizes the Jewish orientation of the institution. The building is closed on the Sabbath and on Jewish holidays. It moved into its own modern building one block north of Lincoln Center in 1978. The Abraham Goodman House, which also contains the famed Merkin Concert Hall, provides the students with the finest facilities for study and performance. There are spacious classrooms, well-equipped instrumental, dance and art studios, the Ann Goodman Recital Hall, an Art Gallery, music library and recording studio. Highlights of the varied concert series at Merkin Concert Hall include Heritage Concerts, Twilight Concerts of Jewish Music, the American Jewish Choral Festival, the Musica Camerit, and the annual "Judas Maccabaeus" Open Sing.

Proceed on West 67th Street to Amsterdam Avenue, turn right and continue to West 69th Street.

Stop 19. LINCOLN SQUARE SYNAGOGUE
200 Amsterdam Avenue

Designed in 1970 by Hausman and Rosenberg, the Lincoln Square Synagogue is designed as a theatre in the round, reaffirming the Torah as the central core of Jewish life. West Siders often refer to the Lincoln Square Synagogue as "Riskin's Shul," in honor of Rabbi Shlomo Riskin who has provided specifically designed educational and social programs for young adults who have little or no Jewish background. On a typical Sabbath, services begin at 7:50 A.M. with the "Hashkamah" minyan, designed for early risers. That service is followed by kiddush and a lecture. At 8:30 A.M., there are morning services in the main sanctuary. At 9:15 A.M., there is a service for people with little or no religious background. At 9:45 A.M., there is one additional service for late risers, which is known as the "Chulent" minyan, since, after the service, a kiddush with a piping-hot caldron of chulent is served. The Lincoln Square Synagogue provides a "hospitality" service for people wishing to stay on the Upper West Side for Sabbath. For information, call 874-6100.

Detour
Stop 20. CONGREGATION EZRAT ISRAEL
339 West 47th Street

This congregation is known as the "Actor's Temple." Broadway, movie, and television stars attend services in this synagogue. Among the most interesting items in this synagogue are the caricatures of some of the many Jewish actors who have attended services in this congregation. There are daily evening services at 5:30 P.M. For further information call 245-6975.

 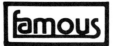

Driving Tour #5
MORNINGSIDE HEIGHTS/HARLEM

Stop 1. CONGREGATION RAMAT ORAH
550 West 110th Street

This is the largest synagogue in the Columbia University area.
It also houses the Chabad House of the Upper West Side.

Drive uptown (north) along Broadway to West 122nd Street.

Stop 2. JEWISH THEOLOGICAL SEMINARY   3080 Broadway

The official platform of the Hebrew Union College, America's first Reform
rabbinical seminary, created in 1873, stipulated: repudiation of Talmudic
regulations and most of the Mosaic code, including the dietary regulations,
in favor of the Prophetic ideals of the Bible, less stringent Sabbath obser-
vance, and rejection of the idea of a return to Zion. Many rabbis occupied a
middle ground between radical Reform and unchanging Orthodoxy. In
1886, the Jewish Theological Seminary was established. It was designed to
disseminate the tenets of Traditional Judaism, the original name of Conservative Judaism. Its first president was Sabato Morais. Solomon Schechter, a world-renowned Jewish scholar, was the Seminary's president from
1902 until his death in 1915. Under Schechter's guidance, the Seminary
acquired a reputation for leadership and scholarship throughout the world.
The Jewish Theological Seminary is the central institution of the Conservative Movement. The Jewish Museum is under the auspices of the Jewish
Theological Seminary.

*For a spectacular view of the Jewish Theological Seminary and the
surrounding area of Morningside Heights, Harlem, and the Hudson
River, go to Riverside Church, at Riverside Drive and West 122nd
Street. Take the "tower" elevator to the 20th floor and walk up ten
flight of stairs in the bell tower. Avoid the bell tower on the hour!*

*Continue driving uptown along Broadway to West 125th Street. Turn
right on West 125th Street and immediately turn left onto Old
Broadway.*

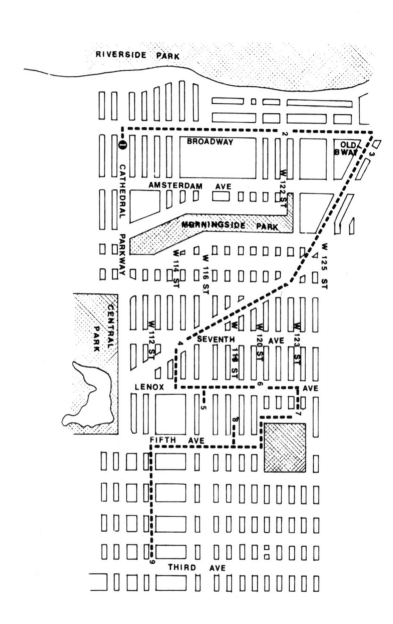

RIVERSIDE PARK

BROADWAY

OLD BWAY

CATHEDRAL PARKWAY

AMSTERDAM AVE

W 122 ST

MORNINGSIDE PARK

W 125 ST

W 114 ST

W 116 ST

CENTRAL PARK

W 112 ST

SEVENTH AVE

W 118 ST

W 120 ST

W 123 ST

LENOX AVE

FIFTH AVE

THIRD AVE

DRIVING TOUR #5:
MORNING SIDE HEIGHTS/HARLEM

Stop 3. OLD BROADWAY SYNAGOGUE

This is one of the last functioning synagogues in Harlem. The congregation is composed mostly of students from Columbia University and the Jewish Theological Seminary.

Drive back to West 125th Street and continue driving eastward to St. Nicholas Avenue. Bear right and continue driving southward along St. Nicholas Avenue to West 114th Street.

Stop 4. TEMPLE ANSCHE CHESED (*orig.)
1881 Seventh Avenue

Organized in 1876, this building was designed in 1908 by Edward I. Shire. The congregation moved downtown, to the Upper West Side, and commissioned the same architect to design its 1927 synagogue building. The congregation is still functioning at West End Avenue and West 100th Street.

Turn left at West 114th Street, drive one block to Lenox Avenue and turn left. Drive uptown to West 116th Street and turn right.

Stop 5. CONGREGATION OHAB ZEDEK (orig.)
18 West 116th Street

The first home of the First Hungarian Congregation Ohab Zedek, which had been founded in 1873, was at 172 Norfolk Street (in the Lower East Side), in the synagogue building that had formerly belonged to Congregation Anshe Chesed (a Reform congregation). In 1908, after many of its members had migrated uptown to then-fashionable Harlem, Ohab Zedek purchased its branch at 18 West 116th Street. The world-famous cantor, Yossele Rosenblatt was engaged in 1912. He officiated in the Harlem synagogue for many years. In the 1920s, many Jews left Harlem and in 1926, the congregation moved to its present location in the Upper West Side, at 118 West 95th Street.

Return back to Lenox Avenue and continue driving uptown to West 120th Street.

---

*The author uses the abbreviation "orig." to designate that the named institution is no longer functioning.

Stop 6. TEMPLE ISRAEL OF HARLEM (orig.)
Lenox Avenue & West 120th Street

Once one of the most prestigious synagogues in the city, this Neo-Roman structure dates from the period when a number of German-Jewish families took up residence in the area's town houses which had been occupied by families of Dutch, English, and Irish descent. Although Orthodox when it had been organized as the Hand-In-Hand Congregation in 1873, the congregation adopted the Reform ritual in 1888, changing its name to Temple Israel. This building was designed by the Jewish architect, Arnold Brunner, in 1907. The congregation moved from the Lenox Avenue building in the 1920s, to 210 West 91st Street. That building is now occupied by the Young Israel of The West Side. The final move was to its present location on the Upper East Side, at 112 East 75th Street.

Continue driving north along Lenox Avenue to West 123rd Street. Turn right on West 123rd Street and drive to the corner.

Stop 7. ETHIOPIAN HEBREW CONGREGATION
1 West 123rd Street

The only Falashan (Black Jewish) congregation in Manhattan. The congregants claim to be Ethiopian Hebrews who trace their descent to Solomon and Sheba, and who observe Kashruth (Jewish dietary laws) and circumcision. The congregation follows the Orthodox tradition. NOTE: Tours of the Ethiopian Hebrew Congregation are available by appointment only. Call 534-1058.

Turn right at Mount Morris Park West. Drive to West 120th Street and turn left on West 120th Street. Drive to Fifth Avenue and turn right. Continue south on Fifth Avenue to West 117th Street. Turn right on West 117th Street. Drive to Lenox Avenue and turn right. At West 118th, turn right.

Stop 8. CONGREGATION SHAARE ZEDEK OF HARLEM (orig.)
23 West 118th Street

Originating in the Lower East Side in 1837, the congregation moved to this building in 1900. It was designed by Michael Bernstein. Harlem was a bustling Jewish community at the turn of the century. The New York Times editorial in 1900, described Harlem as a "Jewish community bursting at its seams." There were over 100,000 Jews living in Harlem at the turn of the century. There were over seventy-five synagogues (including shteeblech) and several yeshivas (Hebrew schools). The largest Jewish school in America, the Uptown Talmud Torah (Harlem Hebrew Institute) was organized in 1890 and was located at 132 East 111th Street. That institution is no longer extant. Congregation Shaare Zedek moved to the Upper West Side in 1922 and is presently located at 210 West 93rd Street.

Drive to corner and turn right onto Fifth Avenue. Continue driving downtown along Fifth Avenue. Turn left at East 112th Street.

Stop 9. CONGREGATION TIKVAS ISRAEL (orig.)
160 East 112th Street

Driving Tour #6
WASHINGTON HEIGHTS

Starting point at Broadway & West 149th Street.

Stop 1. TEMPLE BNAI ISRAEL SHEARITH JUDAH (*orig.)
610 West 149th Street

The ornamental reliefs of Menorahs, Lions of Judah, and Ten Commandment Tablets are still present on the facade of this former synagogue which was built in 1920. Also note the exquisite detailing atop the copper dome.

Drive north along Broadway to West 155th Street. Turn right, go one block and turn left onto Amsterdam Avenue. Turn left at West 157th Street.

Stop 2. CONGREGATION AHAVATH ISRAEL
502 West 157th Street

The congregation has just sold its century-old building. The Holy Ark, reading platform, and other religious artifacts will be shipped to Kiryat Kaminetz, a village north of Jerusalem, Israel. That new congregation in Israel will be called Cong. Ahavath Israel.

Continue downhill on West 157th Street and turn right onto Broadway. Drive north to West 161st Street and look left.

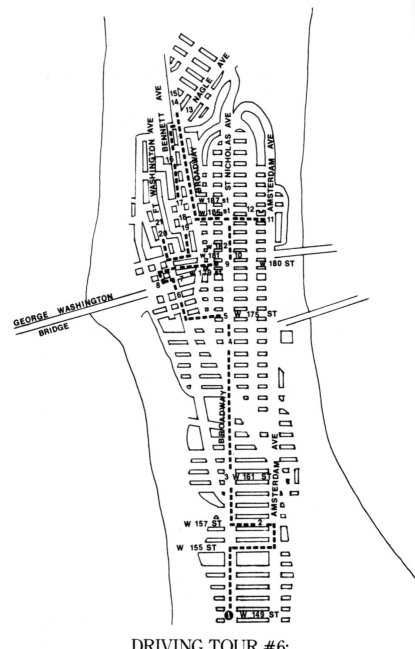

DRIVING TOUR #6:
WASHINGTON HEIGHTS

Stop 3. HEBREW TABERNACLE (orig.)   605 West 161st Street

Organized in 1906, the Hebrew Tabernacle built its first structure at this location in 1922. The congregation moved to West 185th Street & Ft. Washington Avenue, a former Christian Science church, in 1974. The congregation follows the Liberal or Reform ritual.

Continue driving north along Broadway, bear right and go to West 172nd Street.

Stop 4. YOUNG ISRAEL OF WASHINGTON HEIGHTS (orig.) 1250 St. Nicholas Avenue

The four-story brownstone structure is now occupied by a local church.

Drive north along St. Nicholas Avenue and turn left at West 175th Street.

Stop 5. BETH HAMEDRASH HAGADOL OF WASHINGTON HEIGHTS   610 West 175th Street.

Although the area south of the George Washington Bridge approach (West 179th Street) is predominantly Hispanic, this synagogue is still maintained and still functioning.

Continue on West 175th Street and turn right at Ft. Washington Avenue. Go to West 177th Street.

Stop 6. CONGREGATIONS KEHILAS YAKOV & NODAH B'YEHUDA   390 Ft. Washington Avenue

There are two congregations housed in this remodelled townhouse.

Drive north along Ft. Washington Avenue to West 179th Street. Look to right.

Stop 7. CONGREGATION SHAARE HATIKVAH 711 West 179th Street

Turn left at West 179th Street and drive one block.

Stop 8. WASHINGTON HEIGHTS CONGREGATION 815 West 179th Street

This building was originally designed for Temple Beth Sholom of Washington Heights.

Turn right onto Pinehurst Avenue and go one block to West 180th Street. Turn right and continue eastward.

Stop 9. TEMPLE OF THE COVENANT (orig.)
612 West 180th Street

This former Reform congregation is now occupied by a local church.

Continue along West 180th Street to St. Nicholas Avenue. Turn left and drive to West 182nd Street.

Stop 10. CONGREGATION BETH HILLEL OF WASHINGTON HEIGHTS   571 West 182nd Street

Continue north along St. Nicholas Avenue to West 185th Street, turn right and proceed to Amsterdam Avenue.

Stop 11. YESHIVA UNIVERSITY
Amsterdam Avenue & West 183rd– 187th Streets

Yeshiva University is America's oldest and largest university under Jewish auspices. The main campus consists of the following schools: Rabbi Isaac Elchanan Theological Seminary, Yeshiva High School for Boys (MTA), Yeshiva College, Bernard Revel Graduate School and the Wurzweiler School for Social Work. Yeshiva University started as Yeshiva Etz Chaim in 1886 in the Lower East Side. The first building on the Washington Heights campus at 2540 Amsterdam Avenue (West 186th Street) was constructed in 1928 at a cost of $2,500,000. It was designed by Charles B. Meyers, architect of Temple Rodeph Sholom (7 West 83rd Street), in the Moorish Revival motif. The Yeshiva University Museum, housed in the Library Building (2520 Amsterdam Avenue) has, on permanent display, ten scale-models of "Synagogues Through the Centuries"—spanning the 3rd through 19th centuries. A similar display is located in the Beit Hatefustot—Museum of the Jewish Diaspora, in Tel Aviv University, Israel.

Double-back on West 185th Street and go 1-1/2 blocks.

Stop 12. CONGREGATION GATES OF ISRAEL
560 West 185th Street

This building also houses the Rabbi Moses Soleveichik Yeshiva. With the drop in student enrollment, the yeshiva closed its classes.
The building was recently purchased by Yeshiva University.

Continue driving west along West 185th Street, go down the steep hill to Broadway. Turn right on Broadway and bear right onto Nagle Avenue.

Stop 13. YMHA OF WASHINGTON HEIGHTS   54 Nagle Avenue

Double-back to Broadway, turn right and proceed northward to West 196th Street.

Stop 14. JEWISH MEMORIAL HOSPITAL (orig.)
Broadway & West 196th Street

The Jewish Memorial Hospital was closed in the early 1980s because of budget cuts. The building now stands abandoned. Patients are now served by Columbia Presbyterian Medical Center at West 168th Street & Broadway or the Montefiore Hospital, in the Bronx.

Continue northward along Broadway, about 50 feet beyond the Jewish Memorial Hospital.

Stop 15. CONGREGATION OHAV SHOLAUM   2624 Broadway

Double-back on Broadway, drive south to Bennett Avenue, turn right.

Washington Heights contains some of the most dramatic landscape scenes in the city. The steep hills and valleys are generally paved-over with concrete and asphalt, but at points the natural outcrops of Manhattan schist are quite breathtaking.

Stop 16. BREUER BAIS HAMEDRASH   210 Bennett Avenue

This synagogue and yeshiva was built at the foot of a spectacular geologic outcrop.

Continue south along Bennett Avenue to West 187th Street.

Stop 17. CONGREGATION MOUNT SINAI ANSHE EMES
135 Bennett Avenue

Continue southward along Bennett Avenue.

---

*The author uses the abbreviation "orig." to designate that the named institution is no longer functioning.

Stop 18. YESHIVA RABBI SHIMSHON RAPHAEL HIRSCH
91 Bennett Avenue

A unique building, built on piers, allows the lower concourse to be used as a play area for the children of this elementary school.

Continue to the next building.

Stop 19. CONGREGATION KHAL ADATH JESHURUN
85 Bennett Avenue

This congregation is composed mostly of Jewish immigrants from Frankfurt-Am-Main, Germany, many arriving just before the outbreak of World War II. This is the main synagogue of the Breuer Kehilah. The synagogue's Breuer Teachers Seminary for Girls offers a complete course of studies leading to a teacher certificate.

Continue south along Bennett Avenue to West 181st Street, turn right. Drive up the hill to Ft. Washington Avenue, turn right and continue to #524.

Stop 20. FORT TRYON JEWISH CENTER
524 Ft. Washington Avenue

Bennett Park, across the street, is the highest point in Manhattan. Look for the rock outcrop with a marker indicating its elevation of 267.75 feet above sea level. This park was the site of the Revolutionary War *Fort Washington* and is actually outlined by stone pavers.

Drive one block northward to West 185th Street.

Stop 21. HEBREW TABERNACLE OF WASHINGTON HEIGHTS
West 185th Street & Ft. Washington Avenue

Organized in 1906, the Hebrew Tabernacle built its first structure at 605 West 161st Street in 1922. The congregation moved to this Art Deco building, originally designed for a Christian Science Church, in 1974. The congregation follows the Liberal or Reform ritual.

For a truly spectacular view of upper Manhattan and the northern suburbs, continue driving northward along Ft. Washington Avenue into Fort Tryon Park. This park contains the Cloisters, a branch of the Metropolitan Museum of Art.

KOSHER RESTAURANTS
AND EATERIES

IMPORTANT NOTE: Although every effort has been made to ensure accuracy, changes will occur after the "guide" has gone to press.

Particular attention must be drawn to the fact that kosher food establishments change hands often and suddenly, in some cases going over to a non-kosher regimen. No responsibility, therefore, can be taken for the absolute accuracy of the information, and visitors are advised to obtain confirmation of kashruth claims.

The term *kosher,* when applied to meat products, refers to its ritual slaughter. It does not necessarily refer to its preparation (cooking process) in the restaurant or eating establishment. It is therefore recommended that people who observe kashruth (Jewish dietary laws) inquire whether the establishments listed in this guide are under rabbinical supervision and whether the establishments are open for business on the Sabbath.

Bernsteins-on-Essex   *135 Essex Street 473-3900*
Cafe Masada   *1239 1st Avenue 998-0950*
**Cheers   Kosher Italian Restaurant   *120 West 41st Street 840-8810*
Dairy Planet   *182 Broadway   227-8252*
Famous Dairy Restaurant   *222 West 72nd Street   595-8487*
Greener Pastures   *117 East 60th Street   832-3212*
La Kasbah   *70 West 71st Street   769-1690*
Levana's   *141 West 69th Street   877-8457*
Maccabeem   *147 West 47th Street   575-0226*
Jerusalem II   *1375 Broadway   819-1891*
Marrakesh West   *149 Bleeker Street   777-8911*
Edible Pursuits   *325 5th Avenue 686-5330*
Madras Palace   *104 Lexington Avenue   532-3314*
Moshe Peking   *40 West 37th Street   594-6500*
Ratner's Dairy Restaurant   *138 Delancey Street   677-5588*
Lou G. Siegel's   *209 West 38th Street   921-4433*
Verve Naturelle   *157 West 57th Street   265-2255*

moshe peking ⓤ

40 W 37th ST.

featuring a full, traditional

AMERICAN & CHINESE MENU

ORGANIZATIONAL CATERING AVAIL.

for RESERVATIONS and INFORMATION

Call

594-6500

RESTAURANT HOURS: SUNDAY TO THURSDAY FROM NOON TO 11:00 P.M. CLOSED ALL DAY FRIDAY TO ONE HOUR AFTER SUNDOWN ON SATURDAY

MANHATTAN SYNAGOGUES

Lower Manhattan

Bais Hamedrash Chassidei Belz   *255 East Broadway*   (O)

Bialystoker Synagogue   *7 Willett Street*   *475-0165*   (O)

Brotherhood Synagogue   *28 Gramercy Park South*   *674-5750*   (C)

Chatham Jewish Center   *217 Park Row*   *233-0428*   (C)

Chevre Bechurim Bnei Menashe Avahas Achim   *225 East Broadway*   (O)
349-0089

Chevre Yeshuas Yakov Anshei Sfard   *239 East Broadway*   (O)

Civic Center Synagogue   *49 White Street*   *966-7141*   (O)

Community Synagogue Center   *325 East 6th Street*   *473-3665*   (O)

Congregation Adas Bnai Israel   *257 East Broadway*   (O)

Congregation Agudath Israel Youth of Manhattan   *233 East*   (O)
Broadway

Congregation Anshei Libovneh Villin– Shomer Shabbos   *237 East*   (O)
Broadway

Congregation Anshe Tashkanveh   *241 East Broadway*   (O)

Congregation Beth Hachasidim de Polen   *233 East Broadway*   (O)
OR3-5191

Congregation Beth Hamedrash Hagadol   *60 Norfolk Street*   (O)
674-3330

Congregation Beth Simchat Torah   *57 Bethune Street*   *929-9498*   (T)

Congregation Beth Tomchei Torah V'Ziknei Yisroel   *25 Willett Street*
673-8500   (O)

Congregation Bnei Jeshurun Anshe Lubz   *14 Eldridge Street*   (O)

Congregation Chasam Sopher   *8 Clinton Street*   (O)

Congregation Derech Amuno   *53 Charles Street*   *242-6425*   (O)

Congregation Erste Lutowisker   *262 Delancey Street*   *982-0007*

Congregation Etz Chaim Anshe Volozin   *209 Madison Street*   (O)

Congregation Massas Benjamin Anshe Podhajce   *108 East 1st Street* (O)

Conservative Synagogue of Fifth Avenue   *11 East 11th Street*   (C)
929-6954

Downtown Talmud Torah Synagogue   *142 Broome Street*   (O)

First Roumanian-American Congregation   *89 Rivington Street*   (O)
673-2835

Sieniawer Congregation   *217 Henry Street*   (O)

Town & Village Conservative Synagogue   *334 East 14th Street*   (C)
677-8090

Village Temple   *33 East 12th Street*   *674-2340*   (R)

Wall Street Synagogue   *47 Beekman Street*   *BA7-7800*   (O)

Washington Market Synagogue   *410 West 14th Street*   *243-2507* (O)

Young Israel of Fifth Avenue   *3 West 16th Street*   *929-1525*   (O)

Young Israel of Manhattan   *225 East Broadway*   *732-0966*   (O)

Midtown

Congregation Beth Israel   *347 West 34th Street*   *279-0016*   (O)

Congregation Emunath Israel   *236 West 23rd Street*   *242-9882* (O)

Congregation Ezrat Israel (Actor's Temple)   *339 West* 47 St. (C)
47th Street   *245-6975*

Congregation Talmud Torah Adereth El   *135 East 29th Street*   (O)
685-0241

Congregation Tel Aviv (The Little Synagogue)   *27 East 20th Street*
475-7081

Congregation Zichron Moshe   *342 East 20th Street*   *475-9330*

East End Temple   *398 Second Avenue*   *254-8518*   (R)

Fifth Avenue Jewish Center   *18 East 31st Street*   *684-1374*

Friends of Bellevue Hospital Synagogue   *1st Avenue &*
East 27th Street   *685-1376*

Fur Center Synagogue   *228 West 29th Street*   *560-9236*   (O)

Garment Center Congregation   *205 West 40th Street*   *391-6966*   (O)

Metropolitan Synagogue of New York   *40 East 35th Street*   (R)
679-8580

Millinery Center Synagogue   *1025 Avenue of the Americas*   (C)
921-1580

Radio City Synagogue   *49 West 47th Street*   *581-2839*

Sutton Place Synagogue   *225 East 51st Street*   *593-3300*   (C)

Upper East Side

Central Synagogue   123 East 55th Street   838-5122   (R)

Congregation Bnai Israel   *335 East 77th Street*   *570-6650*   (O)

Congregation Kehilath Jeshurun   *125 East 85th Street*   *427-1000*   (O)

Congregation Orach Chaim   *1459 Lexington Avenue*   *722-6566* (O)

Congregation Zichron Ephraim   *164 East 68th Street*   *737-6900*   (O)

East 55th Street Conservative Synagogue   *308 East 55th Street*   (C)
752-1200

Fifth Avenue Synagogue   *5 East 62nd Street*   *838-2122*   (O)

Park Avenue Synagogue   *50 East 87th Street*   *369-2600* (C)

Park East Synagogue   *163 East 67th Street*   *737-6900*   (O)

Temple Emanu-El   *1 East 65th Street*   *744-1400*   (R)

Temple Israel of New York   *112 East 75th Street*   *249-5000*   (R)

Temple Shaaray Tefila   *250 East 79th Street*   *535-8008*   (R)

Yorkville Synagogue   *352 East 78th Street*   *249-0766*   (O)

Upper West Side

American Congregation of Jews from Austria   *118 West 95th Street*
633-1920   (O)

Beth Israel Center   *264 West 91st Street*   (O)

Congregation Ahavath Chesed   *309 West 89th Street*   *724-8065* (O)

Congregation Bnai Israel Chaim   *353 West 84th Street*   *874-0644* (O)

Congregation Bnai Jeshurun   *270 West 89th Street*   *787-7600* (C)

Congregation Habonim   *44 West 66th Street*   *787-5347*   (R)

Congregation Kahal Minchas Chinuch   *321 West 100th Street*   (O)

Congregation Kehilat Israel Chofetz Chaim   *310 West 103rd Street* (O)
222-3787

Congregation Kehilath Jacob   *305 West 79th Street (Shlomo*
Carlbach, Rabbi)   (O)

Congregation Kol Israel   *865 West End Avenue*   (O)

Congregation Morya   *2228 Broadway*   *724-6909*   (O)

Congregation Ohab Zedek   *118 West 95th Street*   *749-5150*   (O)

Congregation Ohav Sholom   *270 West 84th Street*   *877-5850* (O)

Congregation Ramath Orah   *550 West 110th Street*   *222-2470* (O)

Congregation Rodeph Sholom   *7 West 83rd Street*   *362-8800* (R)

Congregation Shaare Torah   *15A West 73rd Street*   *874-6322* (O)

Congregation Shaare Zedek   *212 West 93rd Street*   *874-3615* (C)

Congregation Shearith Israel   *8 West 70th Street*   *873-0300* (O)

Commandment Keepers Ethiopian Hebrew Congregation   *1 West*
123rd Street   *534-1058*   (O)

Jewish Center   *131 West 86th Street*   *724-2700*   (O)

Lincoln Square Synagogue   *200 Amsterdam Avenue*   *874-6100* (O)

Old Broadway Synagogue   *15 Old Broadway*   *MO2-8086* (O)

Society for the Advancement of Judaism (Reconstructionist)   *15 West*
86th Street   *724-7000*

Stephen Wise Free Synagogue   *30 West 68th Street*   *877-4050* (R)

Temple Ansche Chesed   *251 West 100th Street*   *865-0600* (C)

West Side Institutional Synagogue   *122 West 76th Street* (O)
877-7652

Washington Heights

Beth Am   *178 Bennett Avenue*   *927-2230*   (O)

Congregation Ahavath Israel   *502 West 157th Street*   *WA7-5696*

Congregation Beth Hamedrash Hagadol of Washington Heights   *610 West 175th Street*   *927-6000*   (O)

Congregation Beth Hamedrash of Inwood   *1781 Riverside Drive*   (O)   *567-9776*

Congregation Beth Hillel of Washington Heights   *571 West 182nd Street*   (O)   *568-3933*

Congregation K'hal Adath Jeshurun   *536 West 187th Street*   *923-3582*   (O)

Congregation Mount Sinai Anshe Emes   *135 Bennett Avenue*   *928-9870*   (O)

Congregation Nodeh B'Yehuda   *392 Ft. Washington Avenue*   (O)

Congregation Ohav Sholaum   *4624 Broadway*   *567-0900*   (O)

Congregation Shaare Hatikvah   *711 West 179th Street*   *927-2720*   (O)

Fort Tryon Jewish Center   *524 Ft. Washington Avenue*   *795-1391*   (C)

Hebrew Tabernacle Congregation   *551 Ft. Washington Avenue*   *568-8304*   (R)

Inwood Hebrew Congregation   *111 Vermilyea Avenue*   (C)   *569-4010*

Inwood Jewish Center   *12 Elwood Street*   (O)

Washington Heights Congregation   *815 West 179th Street*   (O)   *923-4407*

Interior view of the landmark Park East Synagogue.

PARK EAST SYNAGOGUE
163 East 67th Street
New York , New York 10021
737-6900

A Landmark Synagogue...that is more than just a House of Prayer...

* Early Childhood Center
* Day School
* Afternoon Religious School
* Banquet/Conference Facilities
* Hebrew High School
* Youth Program
* Adult Education
* Gym Facilities
* Sisterhood
* Men's Club
* Young Professionals
* Daily Minyan

Dr. Arthur Schneier, Rabbi
Marc Schneier, Associate Rabbi
Moshe Geffen, Cantor

Friday Evening Services
at Sundown

Saturday and Holiday Services
at 9:00 a.m.

MINCHA SERVICES
(Manhattan Business Districts)

This list has been prepared by the Commission on Community Services of the Agudath Israel of America, 5 Beekman Street, New York, N.Y. 10038.

Please call in advance to see if there is a Mincha Service on the day of your visit.

ADP   *42 Broadway, 7th Floor, (Mr. Mirsky), 908-8034. Hours: 1:45 P.M. (5:15 P.M.-Maariv).*

Agudath Israel of America   *5 Beekman Street, Room 910, 791-1800. Hours: 1:00 P.M. and 1:30 P.M. (winter), 1:45 P.M. (summer).*

Bache Plaza   *100 Gold Street, Room 8092, (Barry Geller), 566-6550. Hours: 1:45 P.M.*

Belgo Tex   *209 East 55th Street, 8th Floor, (Mr. Bossewich), 759-9460. Hours: 12:35 P.M.*

Civic Center Synagogue (Shaare Zedek)   *47 White Street, 966-7141. Hours: 12:40 P.M.*

Congregation Adereth El   *133 East 29th Street, 685-0241. Hours: Before sunset.*

Consolidated Edison (Con Ed) Building   *4 Irving Place, 13th Floor, (Mr. Posnic), 460-4627. Hours: 12:45 P.M. (winter), 1:30 P.M. (summer).*

Control Data Corporation   *80 Pine Street, 15th Floor, (Mr. Fishman), 668-6117. Hours: 1:30 P.M.*

Department of Real Estate   *2 Lafayette Street, 24th Floor, (Mr. Taub), 566-7624. Hours: 1:40 P.M.*

Diesse Shoes   *350 Fifth Avenue (Empire State Building), Room 7801, (Mr. Abraham), 563-4020. Hours: 4:45 P.M.*

Federal Minyan   *114 Worth Street, (Mr. Goldstein), 264-4244. Hours: 12:45 P.M. and 1:45 P.M. (winter), 1:45 P.M. (summer), (5:20 P.M.-Maariv).*

First Roumanian-American Congregation   *89 Rivington Street, 673-2835. Hours: 4:30 P.M.*

Fur Center Synagogue   *230 West 29th Street, 594-9480. Hours: 12:30 P.M. and before sunset.*

G.H.I. Building   *230 West 41st Street, Room 716, (Mr. Schwitzman), 556-8121. Hours: 1:35 P.M.*

Globe   *568 Broadway, 3rd Floor, (Mr. Hanon), 966-6022. Hours: Twenty minutes before sunset.*

Human Resources Administration   *2 Broadway, 5th Floor, (Mr. Karlin), 374-6144. Hours: 12:35 P.M. (winter), 1:35 P.M. (summer).*

L & M Neckwear   *35 West 31st Street, 3rd Floor, (Mr. Gross), 594-0176. Hours: 1:00 P.M.*

Liberty Button   *545 Eighth Avenue, 23rd Floor, (Mr. Parnes), 563-3112. Hours: 1:15 P.M.*

Lincoln Building (Newfeld & Bress)   *301 Madison Avenue, 4th Floor, (Mr. Newfeld), 661-1344. Hours: 1:30 P.M.*

Mesivta Tifereth Jerusalem   *145 East Broadway, 964-2830. Hours: 1:30 P.M. and before sunset.*

Modern Neckwear   *129 West 27th Street, 10th Floor, (Mr. Teitelbaum), 243-8552. Hours: 4:00 P.M.*

Municipal Building   *1 Centre Street, Room 517B, (Mr. Stern). Hours: 12:45 P.M. (winter), 1:45 P.M. (summer).*

New York City Housing Authority   *250 Broadway, Room 1010A, (Mr. Peskin), 306-3777. Hours: 1:45 P.M.*

Phillip Bros. Chemicals Inc.   *10 Columbus Circle, Room 1450, (Mr. Wagschal), 586-6020. Hours: 12:45 P.M. (winter), 1:45 P.M. (summer).*

Phillips, Apel & Walden   *111 Broadway, 4th Floor, (E. Weiss), 964-9000. Hours: 4:15 P.M.*

Port Authority Building   *111 Eighth Avenue, Room 1507A, (Mr. Rosenberg), 243-5061. Hours: 12:45 P.M. (winter), 1:30 P.M. (summer).*

Religious Zionists of America (Mizrachi)   *25 West 26th Street, 6th Floor, 689-1414. Hours: 1:00 P.M.*

Republic National Bank   *1 West 39th Street, 3rd Floor, (Mr. Munk), 930-6530. Hours: 1:30 P.M.*

660 Madison Avenue   *11th Floor, (Mr. Klaur), 980-4241 (call first). Hours: 1:15 P.M. (winter).*

Star Composition   *11 West 25th Street, 9th Floor, (Mr. Weiss), 989-1359. Hours: 2:00 P.M.*

Torah School for Israel   *167 Madison Avenue, 5th Floor, (Rabbi Tannenbaum), 889-0606. Hours: 1:15 P.M.*

Torah Umesorah   *220 Park Avenue South, 7th Floor, 674-6700. Hours: 1:30 P.M.*

Transmittal Securities   *80 Wall Street, Room 418, 797-1455. Hours: 1:40 P.M.*

2 World Trade Center   *Room 6882, (Mr. Lew), 488-4898. Hours: 12:45 P.M. and 3:00 P.M.*

Union of Orthodox Congregations of America   *45 West 36 Street, 9th Floor, (call first), Rabbi Stolper, 563-4000. Hours: Before sunset.*

Wall Street Synagogue   *47 Beekman Street, 227-7800. Hours: 1:30 P.M. and ten minutes before sunset.*

West Side Jewish Center   *347 West 34th Street, (Rabbi Kahane), 244-8687. Hours: 1:30 P.M. and 4:30 P.M.*

Young Israel of Fifth Avenue   *3 West 16th Street, 929-1525. Hours: 12:35 P.M. and before sunset.*

Young Israel of Manhattan   *252 East Broadway, 732-0966. Hours: Before sunset.*

MIKVEHS

Mikveh of the East Side   *313 East Broadway   475-8514*

Mikveh of Mid-Manhattan   *234 West 78th Street   799-1520*

Mikveh of Washington Heights   *536 West 187th Street   923-9548*

LECTURE PROGRAMS

by
Oscar Israelowitz

The Wandering Jews of New York City
The Synagogues of Europe

The Synagogues of the United States

The Source of the Synagogue - Synagogues of Israel

Synagogues Around the World

The multi-media programs (lecture, slide presentation, and sound track) are available for your special organizational meetings. For further information please write to:

Lectures
c/o Mr. Oscar Israelowitz
P.O. Box 228
Brooklyn, New York 11229

(718) 951 - 7072

Brooklyn

There are an estimated 411,400 Jews living in Brooklyn, the borough in which half of all the synagogues in New York City are located. Jewish settlement in Brooklyn started in the late 1830s. The two dominant communities were established in the Brooklyn Heights section and in Williamsburg. During that period, Orthodox Jews would row across the East River to attend Sabbath services in Manhattan on Friday afternoon and return to Brooklyn on Sunday. The Jewish communities of Brooklyn have been in constant flux. Areas once considered the "Jerusalem of America," are now wastelands and Jewish "ghost towns." The Jewish communities have basically shifted to the southern half of the borough, except for the two "oasis" communities of Crown Heights and Williamsburg.

1. Borough Park
2. Williamsburg
3. Crown Heights
4. Brownsville
5. Flatbush

6. Canarsie
7. Bensonhurst
8. Brighton Beach
9. Coney Island
10. Sea Gate

BROOKLYN

Walking and Driving Tour #7
WILLIAMSBURG

Stop 1. OUTDOOR CHUPAH—CONTINENTAL CATERERS
75 Rutledge Street

According to Chassidic tradition, a wedding ceremony must take place out-of-doors and "under the stars." The wedding ceremony is quite auspicious. Candles are used as the only source of light. It is quite an impressive site to see hundreds of Chassidim dressed in their *shtreimlech* (fur-trimmed hats) and *kapotas* or *beckishes* (long black coats) lining the front sidewalks of this catering hall. Please note that no weddings are conducted during the period between Passover and Shavuos (the seven-week period of mourning known as the *s'fira*). The outdoor chupah or canopy under which the wedding ceremony takes place is located in front of the middle set of doors leading into the catering facility. Notice the Hebrew inscriptions embroidered onto the chupah—wishing *mazal tov* or "good luck" to the newlyweds.

Walk to Bedford Avenue, turn left and go one block.

Stop 2. PUPA BAIS HAMEDRASH   120 Penn Street

The facade of this synagogue was designed to resemble the Tablets of the Ten Commandments.

Continue along Bedford Avenue to the corner of Hewes Street.

Stop 3. BETH CHANA SCHOOL FOR GIRLS (KLOSENBERGER)
Bedford Avenue & Hewes Street

This Gothic Revival building was originally designed for a local church. In 1912, Congregation Bnai Israel purchased the building. It is presently occupied by the Klosenberger Chassidic sect and used as a yeshiva for girls.

Cross the Highway (Brooklyn-Queens Expressway) along Bedford Avenue.

Stop 4. SATMAR YESHIVA   590 Bedford Avenue

A contemporary elementary school for boys only. The Chassidim believe in separate boys' and girls' yeshivas. Note the below-grade play area for the children.

Look across the street.

Stop 5. YMHA OF WILLIAMSBURG   575 Bedford Avenue

Turn right at Rodney Street.

Stop 6. CONGREGATION YETEV LEV   152 Rodney Street

The main Bais Hamedrash of the Satmar Chassidim has a seating capacity of several thousand. The men are seated downstairs and the women are located upstairs, in the balcony. There are now plans for expanding the existing facilities. The Satmar are the largest Chassidic group in Williamsburg. Their leader, until his death several years ago, was Rabbi Joel Teitelbaum. The name Satmar is derived from the Hungarian town, Satu Mare (Saint Mary).

Walk back to Bedford Avenue, turn right and go one block to #571.

Stop 7. COMMUTER BUS STOP   571 Bedford Avenue

The signs posted on the wall of this building (a former 19th century mansion, now housing the Satmar girls' yeshiva) are timetables for commuter buses which shuttle between Williamsburg and the Chassidic suburban communities of Monsey and New Square, New York (about an hour's drive from New York City). Notice the buses parked along this block. Many of them have curtains in the back sections. These curtains serve as partitions or *mechitzahs,* similar to those found in orthodox synagogues. In fact, these buses are actually used as traveling synagogues. The men actually conduct services coming to and going from work in the city! Since, according to orthodox tradition, men are not permitted to see women during prayer services, the curtains actually function as *mechitzahs!*

Walk one block to Ross Street.

Stop 8. SATMAR REBBE MANSION
Bedford Avenue & Ross Street

The free-standing mansion on the northwest corner houses the present-day mansion of the Satmar Rebbe.

Cross Bedford Avenue.

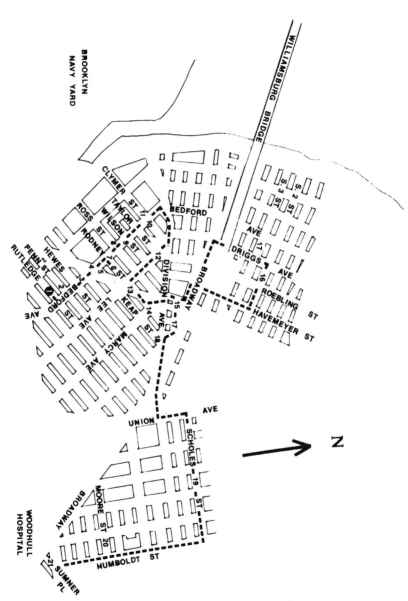

WALKING AND DRIVING TOUR #7:
WILLIAMBURG

Stop 9. FORMER MANSION OF THE SATMAR REBBE
Bedford Avenue (between Ross & Wilson Streets)

The only Neo-Colonial "suburban-style" home in Williamsburg was designed for the former Satmar Rebbe, Rabbi Joel Teitelbaum.

Continue along Bedford Avenue to Clymer Street.

Stop 10. CONGREGATION TIFERETH ISRAEL
491 Bedford Avenue

One of the few remaining non-Chassidic congregations in Williamsburg. Its 1976 contemporary structure replaces the former *shul* which was located on this site but was destroyed by fire. This congregation has a tradition of hiring the world's best cantors. It is reported that Yoselle Rosenblatt conducted services for this congregation in the 1920s. Note the sign on the front door (as an incentive for worshippers to attend services): "We serve breakfast every Sunday morning after 8:00 A.M."

Walk diagonally across Bedford Avenue.

Stop 11. ORIGINAL MANSION OF THE SATMAR REBBE
Bedford Avenue & Clymer Street

Most of the Satmar Chassidim came to New York following World War II. The first mansion of the Satmar Rebbe is still extant at the corner of Bedford Avenue and Clymer Street. Note the *succos* still standing on the back porch.

Walk along Bedford Avenue, turn right at Division Avenue, then bear right onto Lee Avenue.

Stop 12. KHAL ADAS YEREYIM (VIEN)
Roebling & Taylor Streets

Continue along Lee Avenue to Rodney Street and turn left at police control.

Lee Avenue is the main commercial street in Williamsburg. Many of the shops have signs printed in Yiddish. Yiddish is also the main language spoken in this 20th century version of a *shtetl*. There are specialty shops which cater to the unique clothing requirements worn by the Chassidim such as *shtreimlech* (fur-trimmed hats worn by married men on the Sabbath), *shaitlech* (wigs which are required to be worn by married women), and *kapotas* (long, silk coats worn by the men).

Stop 13. RABBI JOEL TEITELBAUM PLACE
Lee Avenue & Brooklyn-Queens Expressway

This street is named after the late leader of the Satmar Chassidim, Rabbi Joel Teitelbaum.

Walk along Rabbi Joel Teitelbaum Place to Marcy Avenue.

Stop 14. BAIS RACHEL   Marcy Avenue & Rodney Street

This former public school now houses the girls' yeshiva of the Satmar Chassidim, Bais Rachel.

Walk to Division Avenue and turn right at Marcy Avenue.

Stop 15. PAZ BUILDING   Marcy Avenue & South 9th Street

A Chassidic-owned construction company, PAZ, has purchased the long-abandoned YMCA building. Plans are underway to renovate the structure into a high-tech office complex. The plans call for half of the brick walls to be demolished—actually cutting a diagonal section through the building. Half of the building would be the original brick structure, while the other half would be a newly-constructed, glass-enclosed, six-story atrium!

NOTE: At this junction, the walking tour becomes a driving tour since the areas beyond this point are in a high-crime zone.

Turn left on Broadway, drive one block and turn right at Havemeyer Street. Continue to South 2nd Street, turn left and go 1-1/2 blocks.

Stop 16. FORMER SYNAGOGUE   199 South 2nd Street

Drive 1/2 block to Driggs Avenue and turn left. Continue for one block to South 3rd Street and look to right.

Stop 17. SITE OF TORAH VODAATH HIGH SCHOOL
141 South 3rd Street

In 1967, Torah Vodaath High School moved to East 9th Street & Cortelyou Road, in the Flatbush section of Brooklyn. The original building was demolished. All that remains today is a parking lot for a drug rehabilitation center.

Continue driving along Driggs Avenue to Broadway, turn left and drive to Rodney Street.

Stop 18. CONGREGATION BETH JACOB OHAV SHOLOM
284 Rodney Street (corner Broadway)

The oldest Orthodox congregation in Brooklyn, Beth Jacob, was organized in 1867 and was located on South 3rd Street. With the construction of the Brooklyn-Queens Expressway and the connecting approach to the Williamsburg Bridge in the early 1950s, the original synagogue building was demolished. In 1956, Congregation Beth Jacob Ohav Sholom built its present synagogue building at the corner of Rodney Street and Broadway.

Continue driving on Broadway for one block. At Keap Street turn right. Go one block and at Division Avenue turn left.

Stop 19. CHASSIDIC YESHIVA   274 Keap Street

In 1850, the first Jewish congregation in Brooklyn was organized by a group of German Jews. Kahal Kodesh Beth Elokim, later called Temple Beth Elokim, followed the Orthodox tradition at its outset. However, with the completion of its elegant temple at 274 Keap Street in 1876, it adopted the Reform ritual. The Hebrew abbreviations of K'K'B'E' are still visible on the facade of the structure. The building was designed in High Victorian Gothic by architect, William B. Ditmars. As a result of the shift of the Jewish population throughout Brooklyn, two of the oldest congregations, Temple Beth Elokim and Temple Israel, were merged in 1921, forming the Union Temple. The Keap Street building was later used by an Orthodox congregation. After a fire in 1979, the interior of the synagogue was gutted and replaced with classrooms. Today, the building houses a Chassidic yeshiva.

Drive along Division Avenue and continue as it merges into Broadway. Go to Union Avenue and turn left. Continue to Scholes Street and turn right.

Stop 20. CONGREGATION AHAVATH SHOLOM BETH ARON
(*orig.)   98 Scholes Street

The cove-domed synagogue structure was built in 1888. The building is now used by a local church.

Continue driving on Scholes Street to Humboldt Street, turn right and continue to Moore Street. Turn right at Moore Street.

Stop 21. CONGREGATION CHEVRE KADISCHE (orig.) 93 Moore Street

This former synagogue was located in the first Jewish section in the City of Brooklyn (Brooklyn was not incorporated into New York City until 1898). Congregation Chevre Kadische was organized in 1889. Moore Street is today a major commercial strip in the Hispanic section of Williamsburg.

Turn right onto Graham Avenue, drive one block then turn right onto Siegel Street. At Humboldt Street turn right and continue to Sumner Place.

Stop 22. FORMER SYNAGOGUE   20 Sumner Place

Across the street from the newly-opened Woodhull Hospital, this former synagogue is one of the last remaining wood-framed synagogues in Williamsburg. The building now stands abandoned.

---

*The author uses the abbreviation "orig." to designate that the named institution is no longer functioning.

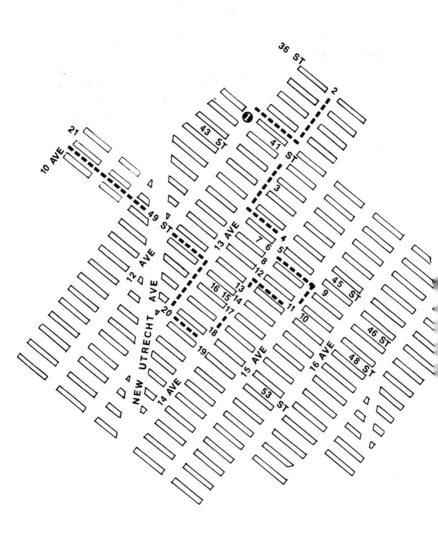

WALKING TOUR #8: BOROUGH PARK

Walking Tour #8
BOROUGH PARK

How To Get There

By subway, take: BMT B Line to Ft. Hamilton Parkway.

Stop 1. CONGREGATION ANSHE LUBAWITZ   4022 12th Avenue

Organized as a suburban community at the turn of the century, Borough Park is today known as "the Jerusalem of America." It has the largest concentration of Jews in the country. It is the world headquarters of many Chassidic groups and has become the home of many recent Russian immigrants. Temple Beth El, the first congregation in the area, was organized in 1902. The congregation built its first synagogue structure at 4022 12th Avenue. The congregation moved to larger quarters in 1920 and sold its original building to Congregation Anshe Lubawitz.

Walk along 40th Street to 13th Avenue. Turn left and walk to the end of the avenue, to 36th Street.

Stop 2. SHMURA MATZOH FACTORY
36th Street & 13th Avenue

Many Orthodox Jews eat only hand-made (shmura) matzoh during the Passover holiday. The entire process of the matzoh baking is done by hand (no machines at all) and must be completed within eighteen minutes, otherwise it becomes leavened bread, which is forbidden during Passover.

Walk along 13th Avenue, the shopping center which rivals the Lower East Side on Sundays, to 43rd Street. Turn left.

Stop 3. YESHIVA   1315 43rd Street

Organized as the Machzikie Talmud Torah in 1911, the building has always been used as a yeshiva. It was used by Yeshiva Toras Emes for many years and is now used by the Chassidic Yeshivas, Kesser Malka (for girls) and Zichron Pinchas (for boys).

Continue walking along 13th Avenue to 45th Street. Turn left and walk to 14th Avenue.

Stop 4. FIRST CONGREGATION ANSHE SFARD
4502 14th Avenue

Built in 1915, the "Sfardishe Shule," as it is often called, has continuous daily morning services — from sunrise to noon. In the 1920's, Cantor Yossele Rosenblatt officiated in this synagogue.

Continue walking along 14th Avenue to 48th Street. (This avenue

Stop 5. AGUDATH ISRAEL OF BOROUGH PARK
4511 14th Avenue

Walk to 46th Street and turn right.

Stop 6. BETH JACOB SCHOOL FOR GIRLS
46th Street & 14th Avenue

Continue along 46th Street.

Stop 7. MIKVEH ISRAEL OF BOROUGH PARK
1351 46th Street

There are separate entrances for men and separate entrances for women. Chassidic men go to the *mikveh* each morning before morning prayer services.

Double-back to 14th Avenue, look right.

Stop 8. MACHZIKIE TALMUD TORAH (*orig.)
14th Avenue & 47th Street

Organized in 1911, Machzikie Talmud Torah's first building is located at 1315 43rd Street. A girls' yeshiva now utilizes the 14th Avenue building.

Continue on 46th Street past 15th Avenue.

Stop 9. BOROUGH PARK PROGRESSIVE SYNAGOGUE
1515 46th Street

The only Reform congregation in this mostly Chassidic neighborhood.

Double-back to 15th Avenue, turn left and walk to 48th Street.

Stop 10. BOBOVER CHASSIDIC WORLD HEADQUARTERS
15th Avenue & 48th Street

The elegant world headquarters of the Bobover Chassidim has three main entrances, symbolic of Abraham's tent in the wilderness which was open in all directions to weary travelers. The massive granite and brick structure has an open floor plan on its main level. There are no fixed pews or reading platform. The portable *bimah,* tables, and chairs are moved aside when the Bobover Rebbe conducts a *tish* (Chassidic gathering). There are two levels of balconies for the women and three *mikvehs* within this monumental *bais hamedrash.* The Bobover are the dominant Chassidic group in Borough Park. Visitors are welcome to visit one of the most beautiful *succas* in the city during the holiday of Soccos.

Look diagonally across the street to the magnificent domed structure.

Stop 11. TEMPLE BETH EL   4802 15th Avenue

With the construction of the elevated subway lines in 1916 and the subsequent housing boom, Temple Beth El moved from its 1906 building at 4002 12th Avenue to its present, larger and more elegant structure. The new building, designed by Shampan & Shampan in 1920, was patterned in the Moorish Revival motif. Its design was directly influenced by Manhattan's Congregation B'nai Jeshurun, in the Upper West Side. The main sanctuary of Temple Beth El was designed to have perfect acoustics. Notable spiritual leaders include Rabbi Dr. Israel Schorr and cantors Hershman, Moshe Koussevitski and Moshe Stern.

Walk on 48th Street to 14th Avenue and look right.

Stop 12. MUNKOTCH BAIS HAMEDRASH
14th Avenue & 47th Street

This massive and monumental structure houses the *bais hamedrash* and yeshiva of the Munkotch Chassidim.

Turn left and walk one block to 49th Street.

Stop 13. TEMPLE EMANU-EL   1364 49th Street

Built in 1908 for the pioneer Jewish community of Borough Park, this Conservative congregation is housed in one of the best examples of Georgian architecture in Brooklyn. David Koussevitski is the cantor of the congregation.

Continue walking on 14th Avenue to 50th Street.

Stop 14. YMHA OF BOROUGH PARK
14th Avenue & 50th Street

At the corner make a right turn onto 50th Street.

Stop 15. YESHIVA BEER SHMUEL   1363 50th Street

This yeshiva and *mesifta* (high school) has another branch at 12th Avenue & 44th Street.

Continue walking on 50th Street.

Stop 16. YOUNG ISRAEL OF BOROUGH PARK
1349 50th Street

This building, at one point, housed the girls' yeshiva, Shulamith, before its move to the Flatbush section of Brooklyn.

Double-back to 14th Avenue and turn right.

Stop 17. MENORAH TEMPLE (orig.)   14th Avenue & 50th Street

Built in 1927 as the Menorah Masonic Temple, the building was later known as the Menorah Catering Hall. Hundreds of weddings were held in this facility each year. In 1980, the Bobover Chassidim purchased the building and converted it into the Bnos Zion of Bobov—a girls' yeshiva. The building is now called the Katz Building, in honor of the Mexican industrialist and philanthropist, Marcos Katz. The main catering hall is still rented out for special functions such as weddings and bar mitzvahs.

Continue along 14th Avenue and walk to 52nd Street

Stop 18. CONGREGATION SHOMREI EMUNAH
5202 14th Avenue

Organized in 1908, its first services were conducted in the Masonic Hall on New Utrecht Avenue and 56th Street. Its present building was constructed in 1910. The yellow brick synagogue has traces of the Romanesque Revival style of architecture. The interior, however, was refurbished with Art Deco furnishings. There is an exquisite stained glass skylight over the bimah.

Walk to 53rd Street and look across the street.

Stop 19. SATMAR YESHIVA   14th Avenue & 53rd Street

The Satmar Yeshiva is housed in Borough Park's oldest public school building. The building was used by Yeshiva Toras Emes Kamenitz before their move to 1650 56th Street.

Turn right onto 53rd Street and pass the Satmar Bais Hamedrash on the left side of the street. Continue to 13th Avenue.

Stop 20. CONGREGATION SHOMREI SHABBOS
13th Avenue & 53rd Street

There are continuous morning, afternoon, and evening services available during the weekdays in this synagogue — a true service to the Borough Park community.

Walk along 13th Avenue to 50th Street, turn left and walk to 10th Avenue.

Stop 21. MAIMONIDES MEDICAL CENTER
10th Avenue & 50th Street

Organized as Israel Hospital in 1919, it later merged with Zion Hospital of Bensonhurst to become Israel Zion Hospital. In 1943 it merged with Beth Moses Hospital, under the aegis of Federation of Jewish Philanthropies, and became the famous Maimonides Medical Center.

Walking and Driving Tour #9
BRIGHTON BEACH, CONEY ISLAND, AND SEA GATE

Start at Coney Island Avenue & Brighton Beach Avenue

Stop 1. SITE OF BRIGHTON BEACH HOTEL

Austin Corbin was the owner of the Brighton Beach Hotel. In the 1880s, he publicly proclaimed a wish that Jews would not patronize his new lavish resort which he hoped would become "the most fashionable and magnificent watering place in the world." In March, 1888, New York City experienced the cruelest snowstorm in its history. It was known as the "Blizzard of '88" and devastated the beachfront at Brighton Beach. The Brighton Beach Hotel's shorefront was washed away and its foundations were undermined and exposed. Mr. Corbin, who was also the president of the Brighton, Flatbush, and Coney Island Railroad Company (today's D Line) wanted to save his hotel. He jacked-up the entire hotel, built railroad tracks under it, lowered the hotel onto railroad flatcars and had six locomotives actually tow the entire hotel 600 feet back onto dry terrain! The Brighton Beach Hotel was demolished in 1921. The community is now 80 percent Jewish.

Walk north on Coney Island Avenue and turn left at Neptune Avenue.

Stop 2. BETH JACOB ELEMENTARY SCHOOL (*orig.)
Neptune Avenue & Coney Island Avenue

Originally designed as a bank, the building later housed the Beth Jacob Girl's Yeshiva and is now the home of a rabbinical academy.

Walk along Neptune Avenue to #245.

Stop 3. MIKVEH ISRAEL OF BRIGHTON   245 Neptune Avenue

Look across the street.

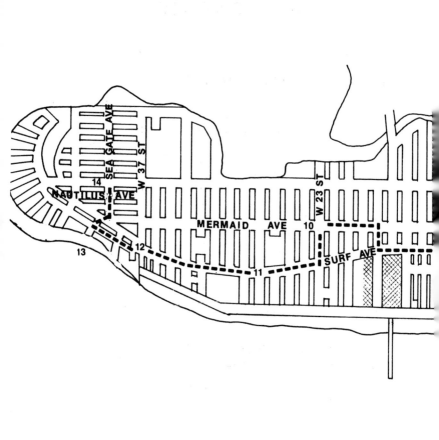

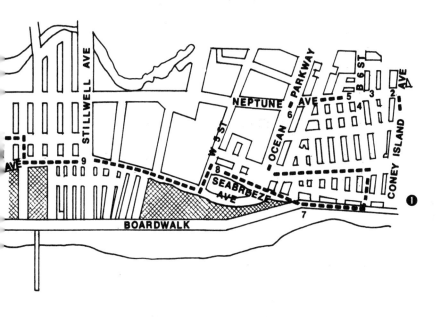

STILLWELL AVE

NEPTUNE · AVE

OCEAN · PARKWAY

B 6 ST

CONEY ISLAND · AVE

AVE

W 5 ST

9

8

SEABREEZE AVE

BOARDWALK

5

6

4

3

2

1

7

WALKING AND DRIVING TOUR #9:
BRIGHTON BEACH, CONEY ISLAND
AND SEA GATE

Stop 4. HEBREW ALLIANCE CONGREGATION
2901 Brighton 6th Street

The largest Orthodox congregation in the Brighton Beach area was built in the 1920s. On the first day of Rosh Hashana (New Year), the entire congregation would "march to the sea" for the Tashlich prayers.

Continue walking on Neptune Avenue to #293.

Stop 5. YESHIVA OF BRIGHTON BEACH   293 Neptune Avenue

This building also houses the Young Israel of Brighton-Beach which was originally located at Brighton 7th Street & Neptune Avenue. That building is now a *bais hamedrash.*

Continue walking on Neptune Avenue to Ocean Parkway, turn left and stay on the same side of the street.

Stop 6. BRIGHTON BEACH JEWISH CENTER
2915 Ocean Parkway

This synagogue is designed as an Italianate villa.

Turn left at Brighton Beach Avenue, the commercial thoroughfare of the Brighton Beach area. Notice the variety of kosher stores as well as the signs printed in Russian. Turn right at Brighton 6th Street and continue walking to the boardwalk. Walk on the boardwalk and turn right.

Stop 7. THE BOARDWALK

Brighton Beach is the home of several thousand newly-arrived Russian Jews. Many congregate along the boardwalk. They have nicknamed the area "Odessa-by-the-Sea." There are several restaurants along the Boardwalk that specialize in Russian cuisine. The Boardwalk extends from Brighton Beach, past Coney Island, and continues up to Sea Gate, a total of three and a half miles.

Walk west along the Boardwalk (toward Coney Island) to Sea Breeze Avenue.

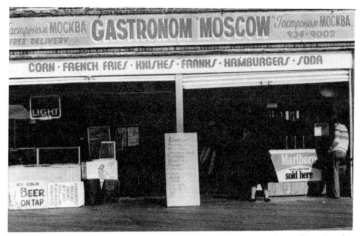

Brighton Beach Boardwalk. Russian restaurant at Brighton Beach, also known as "Odessa-by-the-Sea."

Stop 8. CONGREGATION GEMILAS CHESED (SEA BREEZE JEWISH CENTER   311 Sea Breeze Avenue

In the 19th century, during the hot summer months, city residents flocked to Brooklyn's seashore areas — to Brighton, Bath, and Coney Island Beaches. After the season, the "summer" synagogues would close as the Jewish community returned to New York. At the turn of the century, however, people realized that the beauties of the area could be enjoyed year-round and developed the communities, along with their synagogues, into permanent establishments. The first synagogue structure, still extant, but no longer used, was built at 311 Sea Breeze Avenue in 1901.

At this point, walking tour changes to driving tour.
Turn left at West 5th Street and drive to Stillwell Avenue.

Stop 9. NATHAN'S FAMOUS HOT DOG STAND

Nathan Handwerker managed a small downtown Manhattan restaurant. In 1916, he opened a hot dog stand, pioneering the nickel hot dog. Within a year, the New York City subway, which also cost a nickel at the time, opened its terminal station directly across from Nathan's. Today, Nathan's is a landmark. For many years political candidates for city, state, and even national office have included Nathan's in their New York vote-gathering itinerary. Nathan's does not serve kosher food products.

Drive west on Surf Avenue to West 17th Street. Turn right at West 17th Street and continue to Mermaid Avenue. Turn left on Mermaid Avenue and continue driving to West 23rd Street.

Stop 10. CONGREGATION SHAARE ZEDEK
2301 Mermaid Avenue

The old Congregation Shaare Zedek was the largest synagogue in Coney Island. It now stands amidst the rubble of deteriorating structures of the once vibrant Jewish community. It was built in 1917 but now stands abandoned. The last services were conducted in 1980.

Turn left on West 23rd Street and drive one block to Surf Avenue. Turn right on Surf Avenue and continue driving to West 28th Street.

Stop 11. YOUNG ISRAEL OF CONEY ISLAND   2801 Surf Avenue

The last surviving synagogue in Coney Island is housed in this one-story brick building. All of the windows have been closed-up — an attempt to prevent the vandals in the area from breaking and entering into the humble synagogue.

Continue driving west on Surf Avenue to West 37th Street.

Stop 12. SEA GATE — MAIN ENTRANCE (TOLL HOUSE)

Entry into this private residential community is via a resident's or visitor's pass only. It is not open to the public. There is a wall at Sea Gate which protects the residents of this private community against the "elements" outside, in Coney Island. This wall is similar (in theory) to the wall which protected the settlers of New Amsterdam against Indian and British attacks in the seventeenth century. The main gate at Sea Gate serves as a "checkpoint Charlie," screening all people who enter the area. Originally, Sea Gate was the exclusive and "restricted" Atlantic Yacht Club at Norton's Point (Jews were not permitted entry). Sea Gate is today 60 per cent Jewish.

If you cannot enter, turn left at West 37th Street, drive one block to the Boardwalk and look right, at the Sea Gate Beach.

Stop 9. WORLD WAR II BUNKERS

On the Sea Gate beachfront stand two concrete bunkers, constructed during World War II. These were part of the "shore batteries," which spanned strategic locations along the southern shores of Long Island, Queens, and Brooklyn. Atop each bunker was a large anti-aircraft gun. They were designed to protect the coast against Nazi infiltration. (The Nazis did, however, land spies at Montauk Point at the Eastern tip of Long Island. They were dropped off from U-Boats.)

If you manage to enter Sea Gate ... drive to Nautilus Avenue.

Stop 10. CONGREGATION KNESES ISRAEL
3803 Nautilus Avenue

The largest of the six Jewish congregations in Sea Gate, Kneses Israel, was built in 1924. Sea Gate has a yeshiva and Jewish Community Center. Several Chassidic sects have recently moved into this community. There are no churches in Sea Gate.

Driving Tour #10
CROWN HEIGHTS AND BROWNSVILLE

Stop 1. BROOKLYN JEWISH CENTER   667 Eastern Parkway

The second Jewish center in the United States, the Brooklyn Jewish Center was a direct outgrowth of Manhattan's Jewish Center, which had been built in 1919. Containing facilities for religious, cultural, social, and athletic activities, it was built at the then-staggering cost of $1 million. Notable spiritual leaders included the late Rabbi, Dr. Israel H. Levinthal, and Cantor Richard Tucker, who went on to a brilliant career as an opera singer. The building has been purchased by the Lubavitcher Movement and is presently used as a yeshiva.

Cross Eastern Parkway to No. 770.

The Lubavitcher Rebbe wishes L'Chaim (To Life!) to his Chassidic followers at a "Farbreng."

Stop 2. WORLD HEADQUARTERS OF THE LUBAVITCHER MOVEMENT   770 Eastern Parkway

The simple brick building on Eastern Parkway, in the Crown Heights section, houses the world headquarters of the Lubavitcher Chassidic Movement. Its spiritual leader, Rabbi Menachem M. Schneerson, is known to his followers as the "Rebbe." The Lubavitcher Movement was the pioneering force in establishing the Jewish Day-School system in the United States. These Chabad Lubavitch centers cater to the needs of the respective Jewish communities. Its numerous centers and activities throughout the world reach out to Jews of all backgrounds. The Lubavitcher Movement is involved in assisting newly-arrived Jewish immigrants from Russia and Iran. The movement has an outreach program which involves the use of mobile vans, known as "Mitzvah Tanks." The "Tanks" travel throughout the world and help Jews perform mitzvahs (commandments of Jewish law).

The immediate area around 770 Eastern Parkway is an oasis of Jewish life. On certain anniversary dates, the Lubavitcher Rebbe delivers public addresses, called "Fabrengens," where thousands of his Chassidic followers gather to celebrate. The singing and dancing is interspersed with messages delivered by the Rebbe. The Fabrengens are televised live on cable television networks and are transmitted live via telecommunication satellites to radio stations throughout the world. Notable dates of special Fabrengens occur, as per the Jewish calendar on the 6th of Tishri, 19th of Kislev, 10th of Shevat, 11th of Nissan, 12th of Tamuz, and on the 18th of Elul. For further information about the Lubavitcher Movement, call 774-4000 or PR 8-4270.

Drive north on Kingston Avenue to Park Avenue.

Stop 3. CONGREGATION SHAARE ZEDEK (*orig.)
Park Place & Kingston Avenue

This synagogue was designed in 1924 by the architectural firm of Eisendrath & Horowitz, which also designed the Stephen Wise Free Synagogue in Manhattan. The domed structure contains a stained glass skylight with

---

*The author uses the abbreviation "orig." to designate that the named institution is no longer functioning.

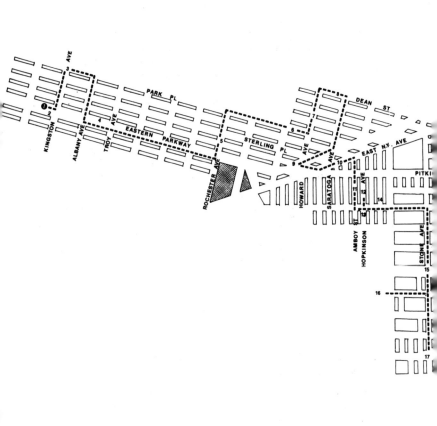

PARK PL

DEAN ST

EASTERN PARKWAY

STERLING PL

KINGSTON

ALBANY AVE

TROY AVE

ROCHESTER AVE

EAST N.Y. AVE

HOWARD

SARATOGA

AMBOY

HOPKINSON

STONE AVE

PITKI

AVE

AVE

DRIVING TOUR #10: CROWN HEIGHTS
AND BROWNSVILLE

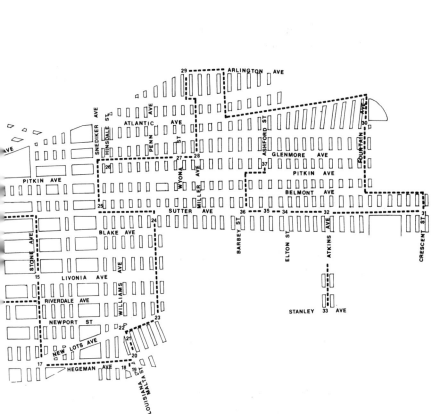

the Hebrew prayer, "Shemah Yisrael," delicately inscribed. Richard Tucker started his singing career as a choir boy in this synagogue. The building has been sold to a local church.

Turn right at Park Place and drive one block to Albany Avenue. Turn right and continue to Eastern Parkway. Turn left on Eastern Parkway.

Stop 4. CONGREGATION CHOVEVEI TORAH
891 Eastern Parkway

Now used by the Lubavitcher Movement as a yeshiva, this congregation was originally known as "Murphy's Shul." The Irish tavern owner donated the land to the congregation in order to erect a synagogue. In honor of his generosity, the congregation nicknamed the synagogue, "Murphy's Shul"!

Continue eastward along Eastern Parkway to Rochester Avenue. Turn left on Rochester Avenue and drive one block north to Lincoln Place.

Stop 5. TEMPLE PETACH TIKVAH (orig.)
Rochester Avenue & Lincoln Place

One of the most outstanding congregations of Crown Heights is presently owned by a church.

Drive north on Rochester Avenue to Park Place. Turn right and continue along Park Place.

Stop 6. CONGREGATION ANSHE ZEDEK (orig.)
1676 Park Place

Continue on Park Place to Howard Avenue. Turn left on Howard Avenue.

Stop 7. CONGREGATION TIFERETH HAGRO TALMUD TORAH
(orig.)   425 Howard Avenue

Drive north on Howard Avenue to Dean Street. Turn right on Dean Street.

Stop 8. CONGREGATION BIKUR CHOLIM BNEI JACOB (orig.) 2134 Dean Street

Drive to corner and turn right at Saratoga Avenue. Continue on Saratoga Avenue to Eastern Parkway. Turn right on Eastern Parkway.

Stop 9. CONGREGATION ADATH JESHURUN (orig.) 1417 Eastern Parkway

Turn left and cross intersection of Eastern Parkway and bear left onto East New York Avenue.

Stop 10. SYNAGOGUE (orig.)   1905 Sterling Place

Continue on East New York Avenue to Amboy Street. Turn right on Amboy Street.

Stop 11. CONGREGATION B'NAI ISRAEL OF BROWNSVILLE (orig.)   97 Amboy Street

The Hebrew name entablature is still visible over the main entrance.

Drive to corner and turn left onto Sutter Avenue. Drive to next corner, Hopkinson Avenue and look to left for Stop 12 and look at the right for Stop 13.

Stop 12. HEBREW LADIES DAY NURSERY (orig.) 521 Hopkinson Avenue

Stop 13. CONGREGATION BETH TEPHILA (orig.) Hopkinson & Sutter Avenues

Continue to Chester Avenue, look to the left.

Stop 14. FORMER SYNAGOGUE   167 Chester Avenue

Continue eastward on Sutter Avenue to Stone Avenue. Turn right on Stone Avenue.

Stop 15. CONGREGATION ETZ CHAIM VECHEVRE EIN JACOB (orig.) 600 Stone Avenue

Continue to Riverdale Avenue, turn right and drive to #105.

Stop 16. CHEVRE AHAVAS ACHIM ANSHEI BROWNSVILLE (orig.) 105 Riverdale Avenue

Note the Hebrew name entablature partially concealed by the cross. The building is now occupied by a church.

Double-back to Stone Avenue and turn right.

Continue south on Stone Avenue to Hegeman Avenue.

Stop 17. CONGREGATION STAR OF ISRAEL (orig.) Hegeman & Stone Avenues

Turn left onto Hegeman Avenue, which joins Linden Boulevard. Continue on Linden Boulevard to Alabama Avenue. Turn right on Alabama Avenue, continue for one block to Stanley Avenue. Turn right on Stanley Avenue. Continue on Stanley Avenue, and turn right on Williams Avenue.

Stop 18. THE SEPHARDIC CENTER (orig.) Williams & Louisiana Avenues

Many of the Sephardic Jews in the New Lots section migrated from Syria to the United States around the turn of the century. Their ancestors had fled Spain during the Inquisition of 1492, settling first in Italy, then in Turkey and finally in Syria. The Sephardic Jewish community in Brooklyn has shifted to the Bensonhurst and Flatbush sections.

Stop 19. CONGREGATION DARSHAY TOV 87 Louisiana Street

Look for the four cornerstones with the Yiddish inscriptions of the congregation's former presidents, vice-presidents, treasurers, and board of directors.

Continue to Linden Boulevard. Turn right and immediately turn left into Malta Street.

Stop 20. SYNAGOGUE OF FRIENDSHIP, TRUTH & BROTHERHOOD KATORIALIS (orig.) 71 Malta Street

This was a Greek (Sephardic) Jewish congregation.

Stop 21. ALLEPPO (SYRIAN) CONGREGATION (orig.) 41 Malta Street

Continue on Malta Street. Cross New Lots Avenue and continue onto Williams Avenue.

Stop 22. BETH HAMEDRASH HAGADOL (orig.) 611 Williams Avenue

Turn right at Newport Avenue and continue into New Lots Avenue. Turn left at Pennsylvania Avenue.

Stop 23. NEW LOTS TALMUD TORAH (orig.) 644 Pennsylvania Avenue

Continue northward on Pennsylvania Avenue.

Stop 24. SYNAGOGUE (orig.)   341 Pennsylvania Avenue

The earliest large-scale Jewish settlement started in 1885 when Jacob Cohen, a textile manufacturer and sweatshop owner, moved to a small town in East Brooklyn, Brown's Village, because of his wife's poor health. He moved his entire factory, brought his workers with him and started a self-contained Jewish community. This marked the beginning of Brownsville, a section once called the "Jerusalem of America." It was a city within a city, with over 300 synagogues, several yeshivas (Hebrew schools), and a flourishing Yiddish Theatre on Pitkin Avenue. Many eminent Jews grew up in Brownsville including Danny Kaye, Max Weber, and Aaron Copland.

At Sutter Avenue turn left, drive to Snedicker Avenue and turn right.

Stop 25. CHEVRE SFARD OF PERRYSLAW (orig.) 247 Snediker Avenue

Continue on Snediker Avenue to Glenmore Avenue, turn right. Drive one block on Glenmore Avenue to Hinsdale Street, look to the right.

Stop 26. CONGREGATION ELIEZER OF EAST NEW YORK (orig.) 133 Hinsdale Street

Continue driving along Glenmore Avenue to Wyona Street, look right.

Stop 27. CONGREGATION AGUDATH ACHIM B'NAI JACOB (orig.) 244 Wyona Street

This was the first home of this congregation. It was purchased from a church and is again used as a church.

Continue on Glenmore Avenue to Miller Avenue.

Stop 28. CONGREGATION AGUDATH ACHIM B'NAI JACOB (orig.) 503 Glenmore Avenue

This was the second home of the congregation. It was built in 1921. Note the Hebrew name entablature above the main entrance and the sandstone Stars of David atop the triangular pediment.

Turn left on Miller Avenue. Cross Atlantic Avenue and continue driving north to Arlington Avenue.

Stop 29. TEMPLE SINAI 24 Arlington Avenue

Organized in the late 1880s as Congregation Bikur Cholim, Temple Sinai is one of only two surviving synagogues in the Brownsville area.

Drive eastward on Arlington Avenue to Barbey Street. Turn right and at Atlantic Avenue, turn left. Continue on Atlantic Avenue to Fountain Avenue. Turn right on Fountain Avenue.

Stop 30. SYNAGOGUE (orig.) 87 Fountain Avenue

Continue southward on Fountain Avenue to Belmont Avenue. Turn left on Belmont Avenue. Continue driving to Crescent Street and turn right. Go one block on Crescent Street to Sutter Avenue and turn right.

Stop 31. CONGREGATION TOMCHEI TORAH 1320 Sutter Avenue

This congregation is still functioning. It is one of only two surviving congregations of an area which once had over 300 synagogues!

Drive west along Sutter Avenue to Atkins Avenue.

Stop 32. SYNAGOGUE (orig.)   308 Atkins Avenue

Turn left onto Atkins Avenue and continue driving to Stanley Avenue and turn right. Look for #858.

Stop 33. CONGREGATION BNAI JONAH   858 Stanley Avenue

The entrance of this little synagogue is at grade but the main sanctuary is sunken, below grade.

Double-back to Sutter Avenue, turn left and proceed to Elton Street.

Stop 34. CONGREGATION CHEVRE TEHILIM (orig.)
512 Elton Street

Drive west on Sutter Avenue to Ashford Street

Stop 35. SYNAGOGUE (orig.)   Sutter Avenue & Ashford Street

Continue down Sutter Avenue to Barbey Street.

Stop 36. SYNAGOGUE (orig.)   Sutter Avenue & Barbey Street

Turn right on Jerome Street or Schenck Avenue and continue north to Pitkin Avenue. Turn right on Pitkin Avenue and continue to Ashford Street. Turn left at Ashford Street.

Stop 37. CONGREGATION CHEVRE CHAYE ADAM (orig.)
Ashford Street

Traces of the original Hebrew name entablature still appear above the main entrance. The congregation was organized in 1913.

KOSHER RESTAURANTS
AND EATERIES

BROOKLYN

Carmel Restaurant   *523 Kings Highway*   (718) 339-0172
Edna's Restaurant   *125 Church Avenue*   438-8207
Famous Dairy Restaurant   *4818 13th Avenue*   435-4201
Glatt Chow   *1204 Avenue J*   692-0001
The Gourmet Cafe   *1622 Coney Island Avenue* 338-5825
Kings Deli   *924 Kings Highway*   336-7500
Kosher Castle   *5006 13th Avenue*   871-2100
Kosher Delight   *1223 Avenue J*   377-6873
4600 13th Avenue   435-8500
Little Jerusalem   *502 Avenue M*   376-9831
Me "V" Me Restaurant   *1521 Kings Highway*
Shang Chai Rstaurant   *2189 Flatbush Avenue*   377-6100
Sparkling Night   *1416 Avenue J*   253-7440
Tacos Olé   *1932 Kings Highway*   339-1116
Tel Aviv Restaurant   *1121 Avenue J*   258-9583
Yunkee   *1424 Elm Avenue*   627-0072

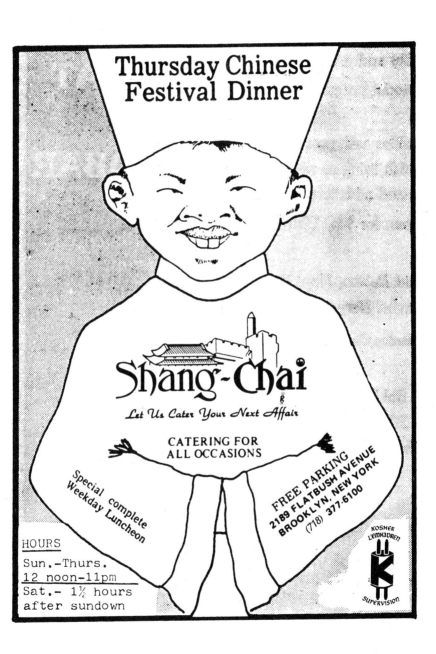

BROOKLYN SYNAGOGUES

Bensonhurst

Bay Ridge Jewish Center   *8025 4th Avenue*   *836-3103*   (C)

Beth Sholom Peoples Temple   *Bay Parkway & Benson Avenues*   (R)
372-7164

Congregation Ahava V'Achvah   *2022 66th Street*   *236-5551*   (O)

Congregation Bnai Isaac   *54 Avenue O*   *232-3466*   (O)

Congregation Chevre Bikur Cholim   *2953 West 31st Street*   (O)

Congregation Lomdei Torah   *2209 63rd Street*   (O)

Congregation Sheveth Achim   *1957 64th Street*   *331-8752*   (O)

Congregation Sons of Israel   *2115 Benson Avenue*   *372-4830*   (O)

Congregation Talmud Torah Tifereth Israel   *2025 64th Street*   (O)
236-9884

Congregation Talmud Torah Tifereth Israel   *1915 West 7th Street*   (O)
DE9-1927

Congregation Tifereth Israel of Bensonhurst   *1835 Bay Ridge*   (O)
Parkway   *236-8283*

Congregation Tifereth Torah of Bensonhurst   *23rd Avenue &*   (O)
83rd Street   *236-6646*

Congregation Tifereth Zvi   *2174 85th Street*   *266-3878*   (O)

Jewish Center of Mapleton Park   *1477 West 8th Street*   *837-8875*   (O)

Jewish Community Center of Bensonhurst   *6222 23rd Avenue*   (O)
236-5551

Magen David Congregation   *2028 66th Street*   *236-6122*   (O)

Marlboro Jewish Center   *2324 West 13th Street*   (O)

Sephardic Center of Mapleton   *7216 Bay Parkway*   (O)

Shaarei Tefiloh   *1679 West 1st Street*   *375-3095*   (O)

Shore Parkway Jewish Center   *8885 26th Avenue*   *449-6530*   (C)

Temple Beth El of Bensonhurst   *1656 West 10th Street*   (C)
232-0019

Young Israel of Bensonhurst   *48 Bay 28th Street   372-5610*   (O)

Young Israel of Mapleton Park   *1400 West 6th Street   256-1060*   (O)

Borough Park

Aitz Chaim Congregation   *4822 11th Avenue*   (O)

Agudath Israel Youth of Borough Park   *4511 14th Avenue*   (O)
438-6508

Bais Hamedrash Yeshias Israel   *1315 54th Street   851-5050*   (O)

Bobover World Headquarters   *15th Avenue & 48th Street*   (O)
436-3479

Borough Park Progressive Synagogue   *1515 46th Street*   (R)
436-5082

Congregation Adath Jacob   *1569 47th Street   438-9230*   (O)

Congregation Agudath Achim Talmud Torah   *865 50th Street*   (O)

Congregation Anshe Lubawitz of Borough Park   *4022 12th Avenue*   (O)
436-2200

Congregation Avreiche Chasidei Gur   *4623 16th Avenue*   (O)
438-8418

Congregation Avreichim Dgur   *1573 51st Street   438-9133*   (O)

Congregation Bais Chaim Yoshua   *4911 17th Avenue   438-9031*   (O)

Congregation Beth El of Borough Park   *4802 15th Avenue*   (O)
435-9020

Congregation Beth Israel   *1424 51st Street   438-9087*   (O)

Congregation Beth Israel of Borough Park   *5602 11th Avenue*   (O)
853-1720

Congregation Beth Joseph   *1324 50th Street   438-9868*   (O)

Congregation Beth Medrash Govoha   *5113 16th Avenue*   (O)
438-9619

Congregation Bnai Abraham   *1415 55th Street   851-9849*   (O)

Congregation Bnai Israel of Linden Heights   *4502 9th Avenue*   (O)

115

Congregation Bnai Usher   *4706 12th Avenue*   *438-8050* (O)

Congregation Chasidei Belz   *4814 16th Avenue*   *851-9890*   (O)

Congregation Chasidei Goor   *1317 49th Street*   *853-1117*   (O)

Congregation Chasidei Ger   *5104 18th Avenue*   *438-8818*   (O)

Congregation Chevre Bnai Israel   *4304 15th Avenue*   (O)

Congregation Chevre Gemilath Chesed   *771 McDonald Avenue*
435-4218   (O)

Congregation Emunas Israel   *4404 14th Avenue*   *535-1142*   (O)

Congregation Hafloh   *4122 16th Avenue*   *435-0813*   (O)

Congregation Hamaor   *5010 18th Avenue*   (O)

Congregation Hayoshor V'Hatov   *1345 46th Street*   (O)

Congregation Kahal Adas Krasa   *1654 43rd Street*   *438-8880*   (O)

Congregation Kahal Adas Yisroel   *4712 14th Avenue*   *633-2305*

Congregation Kahal Chasidei Skvere   *1334 74th Street*   (O)

Congregation Kahal Chasidim of Brooklyn   *4820 15th Avenue*
871-0110   (O)

Congregation Kahal Minchas Chinuch   *1452 55th Street*   (O)
438-8804

Congregation Kahal Ungver   *5306 16th Avenue*   (O)

Congregation Kahal Yereim of Borough Park   *1184 53rd Street*
853-1394   (O)

Congregation Kahal Yesode Hatorah   *4914 16th Avenue*
851-9858   (O)

Congregation Kapitshnitzer Kloiz   *1415 55th Street*   (O)

Congregation Kehilath Yakov   *1137 53rd Street*   *871-0149*   (O)

Congregation Kneseth Horabanim   *701 48th Street*   *633-6378* (O)

Congregation Kruler   *5102 11th Avenue*   *435-2702*   (O)

Congregation Machne Torah   *1375 57th Street*   (O)

Congregation Mincha Chadasha   *1243 48th Street*   *438-8805* (O)

Congregation Minyan Mir   *5401 16th Avenue*   *438-9173* (O)

Congregation Minyan Sfard   *803 46th Street*   (O)

Congregation Netsah Israel   *1535 49th Street*   *438-8813*   (O)

Congregation Ohel Sholom   *4419 12th Avenue*   *854-7240*   (O)

Congregation Ohev Sholom   *1266 47th Street*   (O)

Congregation Oholey Shem   *5206 12th Avenue*   (O)

Congregation Ohr Torah   *1520 48th Street*   *851-1628*   (O)

Congregation Rabbi Moshe Bick   *1545 55th Street*   (O)

Congregation Sanz   *1643 45th Street*   *435-0500*   (O)

Congregation Shaare Zimra   *1550 50th Street*   *851-0100*   (O)

Congregation Sharei Zion   *1533 48th Street*   (O)

Congregation Shomrei Emunah   *5202 14th Avenue*   *851-8586*   (O)

Congregation Shomrei Hadath of Borough Park   *1327 41st Street*   (O)   *438-0066*

Congregation Shomrei Shabbos Anshei Sfard   *1280 53rd Street*   (O)

Congregation Sons of Judah   *5311 16th Avenue*   *851-9828*   (O)

Congregation Talmud Torah Zichron Menachem Levi   *1424 58th Street*   (O)

Congregation Toldos Yehuda   *1437 54th Street*   *853-6777*   (O)

Congregation Toras Chaim   *5228 New Utrecht Avenue*   (O)

Congregation Toras Yisrael   *5311 New Utrecht Avenue*   (O)

Congregation Torath Moshe Jewish Center   *4314 10th Avenue*   (O)

Congregation Torath Temimah   *1575 50th Street*   (O)

Congregation Tzemach Israel   *1353 51st Street*   *435-8602*   (O)

Congregation Yeshiva Yavne   *510 Dahil Road*   (O)

Congregation Yetev Lev   *4514 15th Avenue*   *438-9638*   (O)

Congregation Yetev Lev   *1010 45th Street*   *438-8144*   (O)

Congregation Yetev Lev   *4507 10th Avenue*   (O)

Congregation Ziv Yisroel   *4904 16th Avenue*   *438-9428*   (O)

Congregation Zvi Lezadik   *1431 58th Street*   (O)

Crown of Israel Talmud Torah   *1769 56th Street*   *232-4827*   (O)

First Congregation Anshei Sfard of Borough Park   *4502*   (O)
  14th Avenue   436-2691

Gerer Yeshiva Mesifta   *5407 16th Avenue   438-9407*   (O)

Linath Hazedek of Borough Park   *109 Clara Street   435-8621*   (O)

Mesifta Heochal Hakodesh   *851 47th Street   438-9097*   (O)

Ohaley Shem Yeshiva Congregation   *5206 12th Avenue*   (O)
  435-1639

Saratoga Jewish Center   *163 Parkville Avenue*   (O)

Talmud Torah Tiferes Bunim   *5202 13th Avenue   436-6868*   (O)

Telshe Alumni Bais Hamedrash   *5218 16th Avenue*   (O)

Temple Emanu-El of Borough Park   *1364 49th Street   871-4200*   (C)

Toldos Yakov Yosef   *5323 12th Avenue   438-8312*   (O)

Yemenite Hebrew Congregation Harambam of America   *1260 45th*
  Street   435-7824   (O)

Yeshiva Congregation Belz   *1411 45th Street   438-9068*   (O)

Young Israel of Borough Park   *1349 50th Street   438-1411*   (O)

Brighton Beach/Coney Island/Sheepshead Bay

Avenue Z Jewish Center   *875 Avenue Z   646-9874*   (O)

Beach Haven Jewish Center   *723 Avenue Z   375-5200*   (O)

Beth Abraham   *2997 Ocean Parkway   373-4533*   (O)

Beth Am Center   *1182 Brighton Beach Avenue   743-4442* (C)

Beth Emunah   *141 Neptune Avenue   332-4444*   (O)

Beth Sholom of Kings Bay   *2710 Avenue X   891-4500*   (C)

Beth Torah of Sheepshead Bay   *3574 Nostrand Avenue*
  646-5467   (O)

Bnai Israel of Sheepshead Bay   *3007 Ocean Avenue   332-6231* (O)

Brighton Beach Jewish Center   *2915 Ocean Parkway*

Congregation Israel of Kings Bay   *3903 Nostrand Avenue*   (O)

Congregation Kneses Israel of Seagate   *3803 Nautilus Avenue*
  372-1668   (O)

Congregation Shalom   *3858 Nostrand Avenue*   *934-4790*

Congregation Yereim of Seagate   *3868 Poplar Avenue*   (O)
372-9385

Hebrew Alliance of Brighton-by-the-Sea   *2915 Brighton 6th Street*   (O)

Manhattan Beach Jewish Center   *60 West End Avenue*   *891-8700*   (O)

New Brighton Jewish Center   *184 Brighton 11th Street*   (O)
332-9689

Ocean View Jewish Center   *3100 Brighton 4th Street*   *891-5050*   (O)

Sea Breeze Jewish Center   *311 Sea Breeze Avenue*   *372-9749*   (O)

Sephardic Temple Torah Israel   *60 Brighton 11th Street*   (O)
648-0100

Temple Beth Abraham   *301 Sea Breeze Avenue*   *266-3377*   (C)

Temple Beth El of Manhattan Beach   *111 West End Avenue*   (C)
891-3500

Young Israel of Brighton Beach   *293 Neptune Avenue*   *648-0843*   (O)

Young Israel of Coney Island   *2801 Surf Avenue*   *HI9-1949*   (O)

Young Israel of Sheepshead Bay   *2546 East 7th Street*   *891-6767*   (O)

Canarsie

Canarsie Jewish Center   *965 East 107th Street*   *272-2848*

Congregation Ahavath Achim Anshei Canarsie   *9420 Glenwood Rd.*   (O)
257-9586

Congregation Ahavath Achim Anshei Sfard   *1385 East 94th Street*   (O)
272-6933

Congregation Beth Abraham   *720 East 91st Street*   *495-4480*   (O)

Congregation Beth Israel   *660 Remsen Avenue*   *495-4900*   (O)

Congregation Beth Judah   *1960 Schenectady Avenue*   *338-3968*   (O)

Congregation Beth Tikvah   *8800 Seaview Avenue*   *763-5577*   (O)

Congregation Bikur Cholim Anshei Lubashow   *72 East 89th Street*   (O)

Congregation Bnai Israel of Midwood   *1800 Utica Avenue*   (O)

Congregation Bnai Israel of Starret City   *1455 Geneva Loop*   (O)
642-8804

Guide to Jewish New York City

Congregation Shaare Emeth   *6012 Farragut Road*   (C)

Congregation Talmud Torah Ohev Sholom   *1387 East 96th Street*
251-1430   (O)

East New York Jewish Center   *965 East 107th Street*   (O)

Flatbush Park Jewish Center   *6363 Avenue U*   *444-6868*   (O)

Glenwood Jewish Center   *888 East 56th Street*   *251-5335*   (O)

Israel Center of Canarsie   *1234 East 87th Street*   *CL1-9891*   (O)

Jewish Center of Hyde Park   *8515 Avenue J*   *241-8228*   (O)

Remsen Heights Jewish Center   *1115 East 87th Street*   (C)

Seaview Jewish Center   *1440 East 90th Street*   *251-1900*   (O)

Sephardic Jewish Center of Canarsie   *9320 Flatlands Avenue*   (O)
257-0400

Temple Emanu-El of Canarsie   *9320 Rockaway Parkway*   (R)
251-0450

Temple Hillel of Flatlands   *2164 Ralph Avenue*   *763-2400*   (C)

Temple Shaare Emeth   *6012 Farragut Road*   *444-3222*   (C)

Temple Sholom   *2075 East 68th Street*   *251-0370*   (C)

Young Israel of Canarsie   *1265 East 108th Street*   *251-2600*   (O)

Young Israel of Mill Basin   *2082 East 58th Street*   *253-1016*   (O)

Crown Heights/Park Slope/Brooklyn Heights

Baith Israel Anshei Emes   *236 Kane Street*   *875-1550*   (C)

Beth David Gershon Talmud Torah   *450 New York Avenue*   (O)
765-2527

Beth Elishama David   *1666 Carroll Street*   *773-6910*   (O)

Brooklyn Heights Synagogue   *117 Remsen Street*   *522-2070*   (R)

Brooklyn Jewish Center   *667 Eastern Parkway*   *493-8800*   (C)

Congregation Agudath Israel of Crown Heights   *456 Crown Street*   (O)

Congregation Ahavas Moische   *612 Maple Street*   **771-7365**

Congregation Beth David   *442 Crown Street*   *774-2699*

120

Congregation Beth Elohim   *Eighth Avenue & Garfield Place*   (R)
768-3814

Congregation Kol Israel   *603 St. Johns Place*   *638-6583*   (O)

Congregation Mount Sinai   *250 Cadman Plaza West*   *875-9124*   (C)

Crown Heights Yeshiva   *310 Crown Street*   *773-6520*   (O)

Lubavitch World Headquarters   *770 Eastern Parkway*   *774-4000*   (O)

Park Slope Jewish Center   *Eighth Avenue & 14th Street*   (C) & (O)
768-1453

Union Temple of Brooklyn   *17 Eastern Parkway*   *638-7600*   (R)

Flatbush

Agudath Israel of Flatbush   *1302 Ocean Parkway*   *375-2706*   (O)

Agudath Israel of Kings Highway   *1796 East 7th Street*   (O)
375-1630

Ahava Ve Rahva Congregation   *1801 Ocean Parkway*   *998-0283*   (O)

Ahi Ezer Congregation   *1885 Ocean Parkway*   *376-4088*   (O)

Avenue N Jewish Community Center   *321 Avenue N*   *339-7747*   (O)

Beth Aaron Synagogue   *2261 Bragg Street*   *646-8646*   (O)

Beth Am Jewish Center   *3574 Nostrand Avenue*   *646-5467*   (C)

Beth El Jewish Center of Flatbush   *1981 Homecrest Avenue*   (C)
375-0120

Bnai Israel Jewish Center   *3192 Bedford Avenue*   *258-2748*

Community Temple Beth Ohr   *1010 Ocean Avenue 284-5760* (R)

Congregation Adath Yeshurun of Flatbush   *3418 Avenue N*   (O)
338-9414

Congregation Agudath Achim   *1564 Coney Island Avenue*   (O)
252-7289

Congregation Agudath Sholom of Flatbush   *3714 18th Avenue*   (O)
854-2226

Congregation Ahavas Achim   *549 East 2nd Street*   *853-1959*   (O)

Congregation Ahavath Achim   *1750 East 4th Street*   *375-3895*   (O)

Congregation Ahavath Sholom   *1495 Coney Island Avenue*   (O)

Congregation Anshe Sholom   *2066 East 9th Street*   (O)

Congregation Bais Yisroel of Rugby   *1821 Ocean Parkway*   (O)
 376-9689

Congregation Beth Aaron   *1670 Ocean Avenue*   (O)

Congregation Beth Abraham.   *210 Cortelyou Road*   *435-2873* (O)

Congregation Beth Abraham of Flatbush   *1089 Coney Island Avenue* O

Congregation Beth El of Flatbush   *2181 East 3rd Street*   (O)
 336-1926

Congregation Beth Isaac   *1719 Avenue P*   (O)

Congregation Beth Shnay Or   *1126 East 12th Street*   (O)*258-4802*

Congregation Beth Torah   *1061 Ocean Parkway*   *252-9840*   (O)

Congregation Bnai Avrohom of East Flatbush   *407 East 53rd Street*
 485-1600   (O)

Congregation Bnai Israel of Midwood   *4815 Avenue I* O *763-5500*

Congregation Bnai Jacob of Flatbush   *3017 Glenwood Road*   (O)
 434-8855

Congregation Bnai Joseph   *1616 Ocean Parkway*   *627-9861* (O)

Congregation Etz Chaim of Flatbush   *1649 East 13th Street*
 339-4886   (O)

Congregation Hasachdis Yereim   *1201 East 9th Street*   *258-1370*   (O)

Congregation Kahal Kenesseth Israel   *1420 Ocean Parkway*   (O)

Congregation Kahal Sasregen   *1279 East 24th Street*   (O)

Congregation Machne Israel   *2413 East 23rd Street*   *DE2-8788*   (O)

Congregation of the House of Israel   *866 Clarkson Avenue*
 756-6300

Congregation Ohel Moshe Chevre Tehilim Lubavitch   *843 Ocean*   (O)
 Parkway   859-7600

Congregation Petach Tikvah   *971 East 10th Street*   (O)

Congregation Pri Etz Chaim   *2600 Ocean Parkway*   *743-5533*   (O)

Congregation Rozenoyer Adas Kdeishim   *1510 Ocean Parkway*   (O)

Congregation Shaare Israel   *810 East 49th Street*   *629-0476*   (O)

Congregation Shaare Sholom   *1704 East 4th Street*   *339-2796* (O)

Congregation Sheves Achim   *1184 East 14th Street*   *252-1998*   (O)

Congregation Talmud Torah Ahavath Achim   *1741 East 3rd Street* (O)
375-3895

Congregation Talmud Torah of Flatbush   *1305 Coney Island Avenue*   (O)
377-2528

Congregation Tomchei Torah of New York   *1966 Ocean Avenue*   (O)
627-9821

Congregation Yeshiva Rabbi Mayer Simcha Hacohen   *289 East
53rd Street*   *385-7100*   (O)

Congregation Yeshurun Adas Israel   *1454 Ocean Parkway*   (O)
375-9292

East Midwood Jewish Center   *1625 Ocean Avenue*   *338-3800* (C)

Flatbush Jewish Center   *500 Church Avenue*   *871-5200*   (C)

Jewish Center Nachlath Zion   *2201 East 23rd Street*   *648-4865* (O)

Jewish Center of Hyde Park   *779 East 49th Street*   (O)

Jewish Communal Center   *1302 Avenue I*   *258-3777*   (C)

Kings Highway Jewish Center   *1202 Avenue P*   *645-9000*   (C)

Kingsway Jewish Center   *2902 Kings Highway*   *258-3344*   (O)

Kol Israel Congregation   *3211 Bedford Avenue*   (O)

Madison Jewish Center   *2989 Nostrand Avenue*   (C)

Marine Park Jewish Center   *3311 Avenue S*   *376-5200*   (O)

Ocean Avenue Jewish Center   *2600 Ocean Avenue*   *743-5533*   (O)

Ocean Parkway Jewish Center   *550 Ocean Parkway*   *436-4900*   (C)

Progressive Shaari Zedek Synagogue   *1395 Ocean Avenue*   (R)
377-1818

Prospect Park Temple Isaac   *1419 Dorchester Road*   *284-8032* (O)

Shaare Zion Congregation   *2030 Ocean Parkway*   *376-0009* (O)

Shellbank Jewish Center   *2121 Bragg Street*   *891-8666*   (C)

Shore Park Jewish Center   *2959 Avenue Y*   *648-2900* (C)

Temple Beth Emeth of Flatbush   *83 Marlboro Road*   *282-1596*   (R)

Young Israel of Avenue J   *1721 Avenue J*   *338-2056* (O)

Young Israel of Avenue K   *2818 Avenue K*   *258-6666*   (O)

Young Israel of Avenue U   *2119 Homecrest Avenue*   *375-6942* (O)
Young Israel of Bedford Bay   *2114 Brown Street*   *332-4120* (O)
Young Israel of Flatbush   *1012 Avenue I*   *377-4400* (O)
Young Israel of Kensington   *305 Church Avenue*   *871-4543* (O)
Young Israel of Midwood   *1700 Ocean Avenue*   *253-7456* (O)
Young Israel of Ocean Parkway   *1781 Ocean Parkway* (O)
  376-6305
Young Israel of Prospect Park   *2170 Bedford Avenue*   *287-9432* (O)
Youth of Israel Synagogue   *1721 Avenue J*   *338-2056* (O)

Williamsburg

Adas Yereim   *27 Lee Avenue*   *384-9864* (O)
Ahavath Israel of Greenpoint   *108 Noble Street*   *383-8475* (O)
Ateres Eliezer Bicsad   *129 Hooper Street*   *384-8302* (O)
Congregation Arugath Habosem   *559 Bedford Avenue*   *387-9079*
Congregation Arugath Habosem   *133 Rodney Street*   *782-6608* (O)
Congregation Ayn Yakov   *651 Bedford Avenue*   *875-5102* (O)
Congregation Belz   *186 Ross Street*   *387-9508* (O)
Congregation Beth Eliyahu   *111 Rutledge Street*   *855-0091* (O)
Congregation Beth Jacob Ohev Sholom   *284 Rodney Street* (O)
  388-5589
Congregation Beth Medrash Chemed   *161 Rodney Street* (O)
  384-9300
Congregation Beth Yehuda   *62 Keap Street*   *625-8732* (O)
Congregation Kahal Beth Yitzchok Dspinka   *192 Keap Street*
  387-0044 (O)
Congregation Kahal Raatzfert   *182 Division Avenue*   *387-2217* (O)
Congregation Kahal Tzemach Tzadek Viznitz   *118 Lee Avenue* (O)
  625-8875
Congregation Tifereth Israel   *491 Bedford Avenue*   *782-7212* (O)

Congregation Yeshiva Kehilath Yakov   *110 Penn Street*   (O)
  624-9212

Congregation Yetev Lev   *152 Rodney Street*   *384-7449*   (O)

Talmud Torah Toldis Yakov Yoseph   *105 Heyward Street*   (O)
  852-0502

United Talmudical Academy   *500 Bedford Avenue*   *384-9034* (O)

MINCHA SERVICES
(Downtown Brooklyn)

Please call in advance to see if there is a Mincha Service on the day of your
visit.

Board of Education   *65 Court Street, 10th Floor (Stairwell B), (Mr.
  Cohen), 596-3140. Hours: 1:00 P.M.*

Hecht & Hecht   *26 Court Street, Room 1507, (Mr. Hecht), 875-4700.
  Hours: 1:30 P.M.*

Shawkaid   *228 Livingston Street, (Mr. Mandel), 625-2137. Hours:
  1:15 P.M.*

Transit Authority   *370 Jay Street, Engineering Conference Room,
  (Mr. Baum), 498-4149. Hours: 12:50 P.M.*

MIKVEHS

Agudas Taharas Hamishpachah of Crown Heights   *1608 Union Street   493-2661*

Canarsie Community Mikveh   *Flatlands & Remsen Avenues   763-9821*

Congregation Kehilas Moriah of Sea Gate   *3740 Oceanic Avenue   372-6706*

Mikveh (men)   *2965 Ocean Parkway   891-4286*

Mikveh of Borough Park   *1249 52nd Street   GE 8-9808*

Mikveh — Congregation Arugas Habosem   *135 Rodney Street   782-6608*

Mikveh — Congregation Hamaor   *5010 18th Avenue   633-7724*

Mikveh Israel of Bensonhurst   *48 Bay 28th Street   ES 2-9563*

Mikveh Israel of Borough Park   *18th Avenue 47th Street   871-6866 1351 46th Street*

Mikveh Israel of Brighton   *245 Neptune Avenue   769-8599*

Mikveh — Kehilas Yaakov   *131 Rutledge Street   624-9262*

Mikveh — Young Israel of Bedford Bay   *2113 Haring Street   332-4120*

Ritualarium of East Flatbush   *340 East 52nd Street   EV 5-7707*

Ritualarium of Eastern Parkway   *1506 Union Street   773-8826*

Satmar Mikveh   *212 Williamsburg Street East   387-9388*

Sephardic Mikveh Israel   *810 Avenue S   339-4600*

Taharath Israel of Flatbush   *1013 East 15th Street   377-9813*

Queens

Although Jews have lived in Queens since 1759, it was not until after the Civil War that a Jewish community developed. Jewish peddlers, shopkeepers and a few farmers settled in such areas as Jamaica, Flushing, and Newton (later called Jackson Heights). One section of Forest Hills stands on what was known in the early 1870s as Goldberg's Dairy Farm.

The opening of the New York World's Fair in 1939 and the extension of the Independent subway line brought thousands of visitors to Queens. They liked what they saw and decided to settle in the borough. The 1940s and 1950s witnessed a mass migration from deteriorating neighborhoods in Manhattan, Brooklyn, and the Bronx and the creation of instant Jewish communities in Forest Hills, Kew Gardens, and Elmhurst.

The Jewish population of Queens is estimated at 307,500, including about 100,000 recent Israeli and Russian immigrants.

No tours of Queens have been included in this guide due to the fact that the sites mentioned are several miles apart. It is possible, however, to see the following sites in a day's trip.

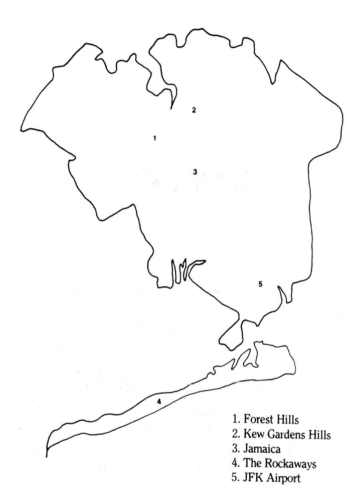

1. Forest Hills
2. Kew Gardens Hills
3. Jamaica
4. The Rockaways
5. JFK Airport

QUEENS

Points of Interest in
QUEENS

How to Get There

By subway, take the IND F or E train to Parsons Boulevard.

FIRST INDEPENDENT HEBREW CONGREGATION (AHAVAS ISRAEL) (orig.)   90-21 160th Street, Jamaica

Jews have lived in what is now Queens before the American Revolution and were doing business in Jamaica, Flushing, and Jackson Heights. Congregation Ahavas Israel built its synagogue near the Long Island Railroad Terminal in Jamaica, in 1905. The neighborhood has changed dramatically, and the younger Jewish residents have long since moved away. The building has been sold to a local church, but the delicately handcrafted ark has been dismantled, removed and sold to another Jewish congregation.

Interior view of the First Independent Hebrew Congregation, built in 1905. The Holy Ark was dismantled and put into cold storage prior to the synagogue's sale to a local church.

129

How to Get There

By subway, take the IND F or E train to 71st Street & Continental Avenue.

FOREST HILLS JEWISH CENTER — ARON KODESH (HOLY ARK) 106-06 Queens Boulevard, Forest Hills

The bronzed ark, designed by Arthur Szyk, offers symbolic representation of the basic tenets and major festivals in Judaism. The entire ark stands about thirty feet in height and is shaped in the form of a silver breastplate of the Torah. Details in the design include the Tablets of the Law, the lion and the deer facing each other, recalling the passage from the Ethics of the Fathers (Pirkay Avot) "agile as the deer and as forceful as the lion," and twelve symbols representing the twelve tribes of Israel.

The Holy Ark in the Forest Hills Jewish Center was designed by Arthur Szyk.

CONGREGATION SHAARE TOVA
84-24 Abingdon Road (Kew Gardens)

Located in the Kew Gardens section of Queens, this synagogue was built by the Persian Jewish community. Initial plans called for a medium-sized synagogue with a seating capacity of about 400. With the fall of the Shah of Iran several years ago and the mass exodus of the Jewish communities in Iran, the congregation now has little room to accommodate these newly-arrived immigrants during prayer services.

The unique lighting design consists of sixty-four fiberglass discs with indirect high-intensity vapor lighting. It's a 21st century lighting design and is quite exciting.

CONGREGATION DERECH EMUNAH
199 Beach 67th Street, Averne

The oldest functioning synagogue in continuous use in Queens, Congregation Derech Emunah, was designed by architect William A. Lambert in 1905. He is said to have modelled the synagogue after the famous Touro Synagogue of 1763 in Newport, Rhode Island, the oldest extant synagogue in the country. The Georgian character of Derech Emunah synagogue relates somewhat to the Touro Synagogue, but the main massing of the two buildings is quite different. The shingle-sided Congregation Derech Emunah synagogue is representative of what the prominent architectural historian, Vincent Scully, has termed the "shingle style." Popular in resort towns such as Newport and Nantucket during the late 19th century, the shingle style characterized many seaside residences and was typical of the Colonial Revival architecture of the period. The synagogue combines the use of shingles with a variety of elegant neo-Georgian details, creating a distinctive and handsome building which is reminiscent of American colonial architecture.

131

Exterior view of the landmark synagogue, built in 1906 for Congregation Derech Emunah.

This synagogue is an impressive reminder of the importance of this section of the Rockaways during the early twentieth century, when the area was a stylish Jewish summer-resort colony known as Arverne-by-the-Sea. The building has been declared an official New York City Historic Landmark.

INTERNATIONAL SYNAGOGUE
John F. Kennedy International Airport

Located in the middle of John F. Kennedy International Airport, the International Synagogue was designed by the architectural firm of Bloch & Hesse in 1963. Designed as a sculptural abstraction, this synagogue blends in well with its environment, where architectural masterpieces have been assembled as a showcase for the international traveler. Some of the architects represented by work at Kennedy Airport include I.M.Pei, Eero Saarinen, and Skidmore, Owings & Merrill. The interior rendition of the Ten Commandments on bronze plaques was designed by world-renowned artist Chaim Gross. The spatial design of the interior closely resembles that of North America's first synagogue, the Mill Street Synagogue, in Lower Manhattan. Under the auspices of the New York Board of Rabbis, the synagogue is intended to serve the needs of the Jewish workers at the airport. There is a Jewish museum with displays of Judaic artifacts from around the world. For information about tours to the International Synagogue, call 656-5044.

The stained windows flanking the Ark were designed by the Israeli artist, Ami Shamir. Noteworthy items in the adjoining museum are the portable Ark which was used in the battlefields of Europe during World War II by the United States Army; three Torahs housed in the Ark have each witnessed a dramatic period of Jewish history. One Torah was used in Ellis Island by newly-arrived immigrants. Another was buried in the Berlin cemetery during the rule of the Nazi party in Germany. The third Torah was tossed atop a chandelier in a Roumanian synagogue in the process of a "game" the Nazis were playing. They had a "game of catch" with the sacred objects of the synagogue! The Torah sat up in the chandelier for the duration of the war.

Another exquisite item in the museum is the miniature silver spice *(besa-mim)* box from Holland, designed in the shape of a windmill.

KOSHER RESTAURANTS
AND EATERIES

Burger Nosh   *69-74 Main Street*   (718) 793-6927
Golan Restaurant   *97-28 63rd Road*   897-7522
Tain Lee Chow   *72-24 Main Street*   268-0960
The Flame Lapid   *97-04 Queens Boulevard*   275-1403
Sholom Japan   *67-05 Main Street*

QUEENS SYNAGOGUES

Astoria/Jackson Heights/Long Island City/Woodside

Adath Israel Center   *36-02 14th Street*   *392-3783*   (C)

Astoria Center of Israel   *27-35 Crescent Street*   *278-2680*   (O)

Astoria Heights Jewish Center   *32-49 49th Street*   *728-1012*   (O)

Congregation Beth El of Astoria   *30-85 35th Street*   *278-8930* (O)

Congregation Beth Hillel of Jackson Heights   *23-38 81st Street*   (O)
899-6666

Congregation Beth Jacob   *22-51 29th Street*   *278-4170*   (O)

Congregation Sons of Israel   *33-21 Crescent Street*   *274-2125* (O)

Congregation Tifereth Israel of Jackson Heights   *31-36 88th Street* (O)
429-4100

Congregation Tifereth Israel Anshei Corona   *109-18 54th Avenue*   (O)
592-6254

Jewish Center of Jackson Heights   *34-25 82nd Street*   *429-1150* (C)

Sunnyside Jewish Center   *45-46 43rd Street*   *784-7055*   (C)

Woodside Jewish Center   *37-20 61st Street*   *424-6762*   (O)

Young Israel of Jackson Heights   *86-23 37th Avenue*   *639-8888* (O)

Young Israel of Sunnyside   *41-12 45th Street*   *786-4103* (O)

Bayside/Douglaston/Flushing/Little Neck

Bay Terrace Jewish Center   *Cross Island Parkway & 209th St.*   (C)
428-6363

Bayside Jewish Center   *203-05 32nd Avenue*   *352-7900* (C)

Bellerose Jewish Center   *254-04 Union Turnpike*   *343-9001* (C)

Clearview Jewish Center   *16-50 Utopia Parkway*   *352-6670*   (C)

Congregation Bnai Abraham   *33-01 Union Street*   *539-7742*   (O)

Electchester Jewish Center   *65-15 164th Street*   *866-4454*   (C)

Flushing Jewish Center   *43-00 171st Street*   *358-7071*   (C)

Free Synagogue of Flushing   *41-60 Kissena Boulevard*   (R)
961-0030

Garden Jewish Center of Flushing   *24-20 Parsons Boulevard*   (C)
445-1317

Hollis Hills Jewish Center   *210-10 Union Turnpike*   *776-3500* (C)

Jewish Center of Bayside Hills   *48th Avenue & 212th Street*   (C)
225-5301

Jewish Center of Bayside Oaks   *50-35 Cloverdale Boulevard*   (C)
321-0300

Jewish Center of Torath Emeth   *78-15 Parsons Boulevard*   (O)
591-4240

Kissena Jewish Center   *43-43 Bowne Street*   *461-1871*   (O)

Little Neck Jewish Center   *49-10 Little Neck Parkway*   (C)
224-0404

Marathon Jewish Center   *245-37 60th Avenue*   *428-1580*   (C)

Oakland Jewish Center   *61-35 220th Street*   *225-7800*   (C)

Temple Beth Sholom   *171-39 Northern Boulevard*   *463-4143*   (R)

Temple Gates of Prayer   *38-20 Parsons Boulevard*   *358-7536*   (C)

Temple Menorah of Little Neck   *252-00 Horace Harding*   (R)
Expressway   *321-1920*

Temple Sholom   *263-10 Union Turnpike*   *343-8660*

Utopia Jewish Center   *64-41 Utopia Parkway*   *461-8347*   (C)

Whitestone Hebrew Center   *12-45 Clintonville Street*   *767-1500* (C)

Young Israel of New Hyde Park   *264-75 77th Avenue*   *343-0496* (O)

Young Israel of Windsor Park   *67-45 215th Street*   *224-2100* (O)

Elmhurst/Forest Hills/Kew Gardens/Rego Park

Beth Sholom Congregation   *97-13 64th Road*   *275-9223*   (O)

Congregation Ahavath Achim   *67-62 Burns Street*   (O)

Congregation Beth Israel of Richmond Hill   *92-01 102nd Street*   (O)
847-1325

Congregation Beth Jacob   *66-02 Saunders Street*   *897-8331* (O)

Congregation Beth Jehuda   *98-39 67th Avenue*   *897-9610* (O)

Congregation Chofetz Chaim   *92-15 69th Avenue*   *544-4662* (O)

Congregation Machne Chodosh   *67-29 108th Street*   *793-5656* (O)

Congregation Mishkan Israel   *67-04 Austin Street*   *896-3077* (O)

Congregation Ohr Israel   *66-20 Thornton Place* (O)

Congregation Shaare Tova   *84-24 Abingdon Road*   *849-2345* (O)

Congregation Tifereth Al   *82-61 Beverley Road*   *441-3862* (O)

Congregation Tifereth Israel   *108-11 69th Road*   *520-9788* (O)

Elmhurst Jewish Center   *37-53 90th Street*   *426-5642* (O)

Forest Hills Jewish Center   *106-06 Queens Boulevard*   (C)
263-7000

Jewish Center of Forest Hills West   *63-25 Dry Harbor Road*   (O)
639-2110

Jewish Center of Richmond Hill   *101-54 117th Street*   *849-2507* (O)

Kehilath Yismach Moshe of Lapish   *90-14 63rd Drive*   *459-2632* (O)

Kew Gardens Anshe Sholom Jewish Center   *82-52 Abingdon Road* (C)
441-2470

Kew Gardens Synagogue Adath Yeshurun   *82-17 Lefferts Boulevard* (O)
849-7988

Lefrak Jewish Center   *98-54 Horace Harding Expressway*   (C)
699-7752

Queens Jewish Center   *66-05 108th Street*   *459-8432* (O)

Rego Park Jewish Center   *97-30 Queens Boulevard*   *459-1000* (C)

Sephardic Jewish Center of Forest Hills   *67-67 108th Street* (O)
268-2100

Sephardic Jewish Congregation of Queens   *101-17 67th Drive* (O)
544-6932

Temple Emanu-El   *91-15 Corona Avenue*   *592-4343* (R)

Temple Isaiah   *75-24 Grand Central Parkway*   *544-2800* (R)

Temple Sinai   *71-11 112th Street*   *261-2900* (R)

Young Israel of Forest Hills   *71-00 Yellowstone Boulevard*   (O)
268-7100

137

Glendale/Howard Beach/Ozone Park

Congregation Agudas Israel   *1618 Cornela Street*   *821-9351* (O)

Congregation Ahavath Achim Sons of Israel   *75-23 67th Drive* (O)
326-7240

Congregation Bnai Israel of Woodhaven   *89-07 Woodhaven*   (O)
Boulevard

Congregation Shaare Zedek   *80-35 Pitkin Avenue*   *843-4840*   (O)

Forest Park Jewish Center   *90-45 Myrtle Avenue*   *847-6273*   (O)

Holliswood Jewish Center   *86-25 Francis Lewis Boulevard*   (C)
776-8500

Howard Beach Jewish Center   *162-05 90th Street*   *845-9443*   (C)

International Synagogue   *JFK Airport*   *656-5044*   (T)

Jewish Center of Ozone Park   *107-01 Cross Bay Boulevard* (O)
848-4096

Laurelton Jewish Center   *134-49 228th Street*   *527-0400*   (C)

Maspeth Jewish Center   *66-64 Grand Avenue*   *639-7559*   (O)

Rochdale Village Jewish Center   *167-10 137th Avenue*   (C)
528-0200

Rockwood Park Jewish Center   *156-45 84th Street*   *641-5822*   (C)

Rosedale Jewish Center   *247-11 Francis Lewis Boulevard*   (C)
528-3988

Traditional Synagogue of Rochdale Village   *165-27 Baisley Blvd.*
525-1451

Fresh Meadows/Kew Gardens Hills

Congregation Etz Chaim   *54-06 Kissena Boulevard*   *762-2323*   (O)

Congregation Ohr Yitzchok   *165-14 69th Avenue*   *591-4726*   (O)

Fresh Meadows Jewish Center   *58-45 193rd Street*   *357-5100*   (C)

Hillcrest Jewish Center   *183-02 Union Turnpike*   *380-4145* (C)

Israel Center of Hillcrest Manor   *167-11 73rd Avenue*   *591-5353*   (C)

Jewish Center of Kew Gardens Hills   *71-25 Main Street*
263-6500

Queensboro Hill Jewish Center   *156-03 Horace Harding*   (C)
Expressway   445-4141

Young Israel of Briarwood   *84-75 Daniels Street*   *657-2880*   (O)

Young Israel of Hillcrest   *169-07 Jewel Avenue*   *969-2990* (O)

Young Israel of Kew Gardens Hills   *70-11 150th Street*   (O)
261-9723

Young Israel of Queens Valley   *141-51 77th Avenue*   *263-3921* (O)

Jamaica/Queens Village

Belle Park Jewish Center   *231-10 Hillside Avenue*   *464-9144* (C)

Briarwood Jewish Center   *139-06 86th Avenue*   *657-5151*   (C)

Congregation Ahavath Sholom   *75-02 113th Street*   *263-1949* (O)

Congregation Anshei Sholom   *85-34 Midland Parkway*   (O)
297-2405

Conservative Synagogue of Jamaica   *182-69 Wexford Terrace*   (C)
739-7500

Queens Jewish Center of Queens Village   *94-34 Hollis Court Blvd.* (C)
465-4993

Sanhedrin Jewish Community Center   *103-06 131st Street*
843-9639

Temple Israel of Jamaica   188-15 McLaughlin Avenue   776-4400   (R)

Young Israel of Jamaica Estates   *83-10 188th Street*   *454-1152* (O)

The Rockaways

Agudath Israel of Long Island   *11-21 Sage Street*   *471-4861* (O)

Bayswater Jewish Center   *23-55 Healy Avenue*   *471-7771* (C)

Congregation Anshe Sfard   *7600 Shore Front Parkway*   (O)
945-4459

Congregation Bais Medrash Ateres Yisroel   *827 Cornaga Avenue*   (O)
471-5346

Congregation Beth Medrash Horav   *15-13 Central Avenue*   (O)
471-3425

Congregation Bnai David   *567 Beach 130th Street*   (O)

Congregation Derech Emunah   *199 Beach 67tn Street*   (O)
643-2288

Congregation Kehilas Jacob   *821 Roosevelt Court*   *327-8007*   (O)

Congregation Kneses Israel (White Shul)   *728 Empire Avenue*   (O)
327-7545

Congregation Ohab Zedek   *134-01 Rockaway Beach Boulevard*   (O)
474-3300

Congregation Shaare Tefila   *12-95 Central Avenue*   *327-7006*   (O)

Congregation Shaare Zedek of Edgemere   *321 Beach 30th Street*   (O)
327-9214

Congregation Tifereth Chaim   *29-04 Far Rockaway Boulevard*   (O)
337-5685

Seaside Jewish Center   *103-00 Shore Front Parkway*
643-1141

Temple Beth El   *445 Beach 135th Street*   *634-8100*   (C)

Temple of Israel   *188 Beach 84th Street*   *634-5064*   (C)

West End Temple   *147-02 Newport Avenue*   (R)

Young Israel of Belle Harbor   *505 Beach 129th Street*   (O)
474-9223

Young Israel of Far Rockaway   *716 Beach 9th Street*   (O)
471-6724

Young Israel of Wavecrest & Bayswater   *23-60 Brookhaven Ave.*   (O)
327-8606

MIKVEHS

Mikveh — Hebrew Community Service   *1121 Bayport Place,*
Far Rockaway   327-9727

Mikveh Israel   *71-11 Vleigh Place, Kew Gardens Hills   268-6500*

Mikveh of Queens   *75-48 Grand Central Parkway,*
Forest Hills   261-6380

The Bronx

The Jewish settlement of the Bronx developed in a series of northward migrations. Although there was a small community in the 1840s, it was not until the late 1880s, with the extension of Manhattan's elevated railways, that considerable Jewish settlement was established.

Driving Tour #11
SOUTH BRONX

Start at the Bronx County Court House at Walton Avenue and East 161st Street.

Stop 1. CONGREGATION HOPE OF ISRAEL   843 Walton Avenue

After World War II there was a mass migration from the South and Central Bronx because of rapidly deteriorating neighborhoods, the construction of the Cross-Bronx Expressway and the availability of good, inexpensive housing in the suburbs. The abandoned neighborhoods were left to decay and the synagogues were usually sold to black or Hispanic churches. The South Bronx today resembles postwar Berlin, with block after block of

1. The South Bronx
2. Riverdale
3. Pelham Parkway
4. Co-op City

THE BRONX

burned-out shells of once elegant apartment buildings. Congregation Hope of Israel is one of two surviving and functioning synagogues in the South Bronx.

Drive East along East 161st Street to Third Avenue. Turn right on Third Avenue and continue to East 156th Street. Turn left on East 156th Street. Continue to Jackson Avenue and turn left. Drive on Jackson Avenue and at East 158th Street turn right. Stop at Forest Avenue and look to the left.

Stop 2. BETH HAMEDRASH HAGADOL ADATH ISRAEL OF THE BRONX (*orig.)   Forest Avenue & East 158th Street

Continue on East 158th Street to Westchester Avenue. Continue under the elevated subway and turn left onto Westchester Avenue. Immediately turn right onto Prospect Avenue. At the first intersecting street on the left, turn into Macy Place.

Stop 3. MONTEFIORE CONGREGATION (orig.)
764 Hewitt Place

Built in 1906, the Montefiore Congregation was among the hundreds of Orthodox congregations in the South Bronx. It was patterned after an Eastern European shtetl (village) synagogue, complete with onion domes. The "penny arcade" style lighting of the archways along the women's gallery was modeled after its East European prototype.

Continue driving south along Prospect Avenue to East 156th Street. Turn left on East 156th Street. Continue to Fox Street. Turn left onto Fox Street.

Stop 4. CONGREGATION BETH DAVID (orig.)   832 Fox Street

This was formerly known as the Fox Street Shul.

Drive to the corner and look to the right.

---

*The author uses the abbreviation "orig." to designate that the named institution is no longer functioning.

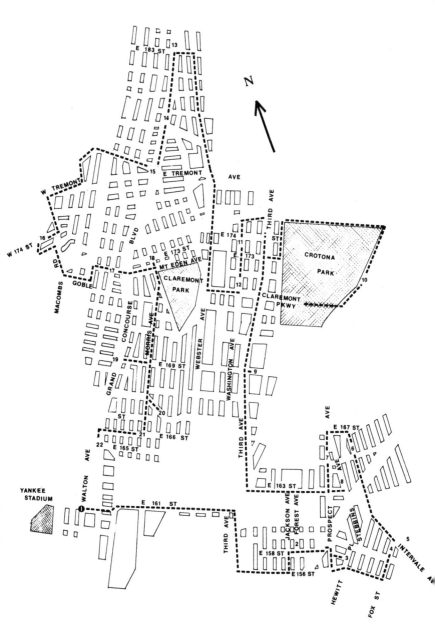

DRIVING TOUR #11: SOUTH BRONX

Exterior view of the synagogue, built in 1906 for the Montefiore Congregation.

Stop 5. CONGREGATION MISHKANOS ISRAEL (orig.)
Intervale Avenue & Southern Boulevard (northwest corner)

Turn onto Intervale Avenue and drive to East 165th Street.

Stop 6. INTERVALE JEWISH CENTER
Intervale Avenue & East 165th Street

In the 1920s this congregation was organized with great expectations. They started construction on a lavish synagogue, destined to be a five-story structure. The lower level was to house the congregation's *beth hamedrash* (used for daily services), banquet hall, and classrooms. Its upper, main level was to house a lavish sanctuary with balconies to allow for overflow crowds. The stock market crash of 1929 shattered all these plans. The congregation started building the first floor of its synagogue but ceased all construction thereafter. Today, all that remains is the basement level of the

145

proposed structure with the bases of what were to be the supporting columns of the Neo-Classical structure. Surprisingly, the Intervale Jewish Center is still functioning! Weekly Sabbath services are still conducted. This is one of only two functioning synagogues in the South Bronx.

Continue driving along Intervale Avenue to East 167th Street. Turn left on East 167th Street. Continue to Prospect Avenue and turn left.

The Intervale Jewish Center is one of only two surviving synagogues located in the South Bronx.

Stop 7. CONGREGATION TIFERETH ISRAEL (orig.)
1038 Prospect Avenue

The congregation bought a former Neo-Gothic church. When the congregation moved, it was bought by another church.

Drive south along Prospect Avenue to East 163rd Street. Turn left on East 163rd Street and continue to Stebbins Avenue.

Stop 8. SINAI CONGREGATION (orig.)   951 Stebbins Avenue

The Neo-Classical facade remains relatively unchanged; reliefs of the

Menorah and Stars of David are still visible. But the congregation has moved from the area and the building has been sold to a church.

Double back to East 163rd Street and drive west to Third Avenue. Turn right onto Third Avenue to East 169th Street. Look to right.

Stop 9. TEMPLE ADATH ISRAEL (orig.)   551 East 169th Street

Organized by German Jews in 1889, Temple Adath Israel built the first synagogue in the Bronx at 551 East 169th Street. The structure now houses a church. The congregation moved to the Grand Concourse and East 169th Street in 1927 and, finally, to the Riverdale section of the Bronx in the 1960s.

Turn at East 173rd Street, go up hill, turn left. Turn right at Crotona Park North (drive around park), turn right onto Crotona Park East.

Stop 10. CONGREGATION KEHILATH ISRAEL (orig.)
1594 Crotona Park East

Continue around park to Claremont Parkway, turn right and drive back to Third Avenue, turn right.

Continue north along Third Avenue to East 175th Street (under the Cross-Bronx Expressway). Turn left on East 175th Street and continue to Washington Avenue. Turn left on Washington Avenue. Drive on Washington Avenue southward to East 174th Street.

Stop 11. CONGREGATION ZERA JACOB (orig.)
Washington Avenue & East 174th Street

In 1930 the Tremont section of the Bronx was at its peak as a Jewish neighborhood, housing 56,000 Jews. It was this growing population which probably necessitated the unusual occurrence of a synagogue building project during the heart of the Great Depression.

Continue south along Washington Avenue.

Stop 12. BETH HAMEDRASH HAGADOL ADATH ISRAEL OF
THE BRONX (orig.)   1590 Washington Avenue

Changing neighborhoods forced the congregation to shift locations. When the Cross-Bronx Expressway disrupted the area, many of the congregation's members moved to the northern sections of the Bronx or to the suburbs.

Continue south along Washington Avenue to Claremont Parkway. Turn right onto Claremont Parkway and continue to Webster Avenue. Drive north on Webster Avenue to East 178th Street and bear left onto Valentine Avenue. Continue on Valentine Avenue to East 183rd Street. Turn left onto East 183rd Street and drive to the Grand Concourse. Turn left onto the Grand Concourse.

Grand Concourse

The Grand Concourse, one of the grand boulevards in the city, was designed in 1892 to provide access from Manhattan to the large parks of the Bronx. After World War I, many upwardly mobile working and middle class Jewish families began moving from the Lower East Side, Harlem, and the southeast Bronx to the Grand Concourse. For a person to live in an Art Deco apartment building on the Grand Concourse in the 1920s was equivalent to being a member of high society. Jewish residents would promenade up and down the boulevard in their best attire on the Sabbath.

Stop 13. CONCOURSE CENTER OF ISRAEL (orig.)
2323 Grand Concourse

Continue south on the Grand Concourse.

Stop 14. TREMONT TEMPLE (orig.)   2064 Grand Concourse

Continue south along the Grand Concourse.

Stop 15. YESHIVA ZICHRON MOSHE (orig.)
Grand Concourse & East Tremont Avenue

Turn right at East Tremont Avenue and continue winding uphill along East Tremont Avenue. At University Avenue turn left and continue driving to Macomb's Road. Turn left onto Macomb's Road and continue to West 174th Street. Turn right onto West 174th Street.

Stop 16. HIGHBRIDGE JEWISH CENTER (orig.)
108 West 174th Street

Turn left at Nelson Avenue and continue to Featherbed Lane. Turn left at Featherbed Lane and continue to Macomb's Road. Turn right

onto Macomb's road and drive to Goble Place. Turn left at Goble Place
and continue down to the elevated subway. At Jerome Avenue turn
left and continue to Mount Eden Avenue. Turn right at Mount Eden
Avenue and continue to Walton Avenue.

Stop 17. CONGREGATION B'NAI ISRAEL (orig.)
1570 Walton Avenue

Continue eastward along Mount Eden Avenue to Morris Avenue.
Turn left onto Morris Avenue and drive one block.

Stop 18. MOUNT EDEN CENTER (orig.)   1660 Morris Avenue

The Mount Eden Center was one of the grand synagogues in the city. It was
the place to have an affair or wedding. The neighborhood had changed
dramatically by the time the building was sold in 1982 to the Bronx
Lebanon Hospital. Plans are underway to turn the old Mount Eden Center
into a nursing school.

Co-op City, the world's largest co-operative housing development, has a
total population of 75,000, with as many Jews as Atlanta, New Orleans,
Des Moines, and Wilmington put together. A community unto itself, it
contains six separate synagogues and an active community center. Many
of the residents are elderly, many middle-class. A large number moved to
Co-op City from the older, decaying areas of the Bronx. Co-op City was
built in 1968 on the site of the former amusement park, Freedomland.

149

Double back and drive south along Morris Avenue to East 169th Street. Turn right on East 169th Street and continue uphill to the Grand Concourse.

Stop 19. TEMPLE ADATH ISRAEL (orig.)
Grand Concourse & East 169th Street

The second home of the Bronx's oldest congregation, Temple Adath Israel, was built in 1927. Richard Tucker officiated as cantor of this congregation for many years. The building was sold to a church in the 1960s. The congregation, however, is still functioning. Temple Adath Israel is located at West 250th Street & Henry Hudson Parkway, in the Riverdale section of the Bronx. Their 1962 building was designed by Percival Goodman who designed over fifty synagogues throughout the United States.

Just down the street (on East 169th Street) are the buildings that were used formerly by Sephardic congregations and a Hebrew school.

Double back and drive eastward along East 169th Street to Morris Avenue. Turn right onto Morris Avenue and continue south to East 167th Street. Turn left at East 167th Street.

Stop 20. DAUGHTERS OF JACOB GERIATRIC CENTER
321 East 167th Street

Designed as eight radiating spoked wings set at the end of an Italian garden, the Daughters of Jacob Geriatric Center was designed in 1920 by Louis Allen Abramson, the architect of Manhattan's Jewish Center (131 West 86th Street) and the Brooklyn Jewish Center (667 Eastern Parkway). The copper Star of David still appears atop the original 1920 building.

Double back to Morris Avenue and turn left. Continue south along Morris Avenue to East 166th Street.

Stop 21. YEHUDA HALEVY SHUL (orig.)
Morris Avenue & East 166th Street

Turn right onto East 166th Street and continue west to the Grand Concourse. Turn left onto the Grand Concourse and drive one block southward to East 165th Street.

Stop 22. YOUNG ISRAEL OF THE BRONX (orig.)
Grand Concourse & East 165th Street

The building was purchased by the Bronx Museum of the Arts in 1982.

The Salanter Akiba Riverdale Academy is composed of three Hebrew day schools that have been literally merged under one roof; there are no walls between the classrooms of this elementary school. It was designed, in 1974, by the firm of Caudill, Rowlett, Scott, Associates. The sloped roof provides every class space with a view across the Hudson River. The chapel is designed as a theater-in-the-round. Before entering the chapel, students pass a memorial to the Holocaust. The academy occupies the land of an estate where conductor Arturo Toscanini lived.

Guide to Jewish New York City

KOSHER RESTAURANTS
AND EATERIES

Flash Kosher Pizza   *3602 Riverdale Avenue   543-1811*

Liebman's Kosher Deli   *552 West 235th Street   548-4534*

Loesser's Kosher Deli   *214 West 231st Street   548-9735*

Simon's Kosher Take Home Foods   *3551 Johnson Avenue 796-7530*

Skyview Kosher Deli   *5665 Riverdale Avenue   796-8596*

Dexter's Restaurant   *5652 Mosholu Avenue (212) 548-0440*

152

THE BRONX SYNAGOGUES

Ahav Tsedek of Kingsbridge   *3425 Kingsbridge Avenue*   *543-6969* (O)

Beth Shraga   *2757 Morris Avenue*   *295-3160*   (O)

Bronx Park East Chotiner Jewish Center   *2256 Bronx Park East*   (O)
655-9934

Castle Hill Jewish Community Center   *486 Howe Avenue*   *892-2372*   (O)

Chevre Machzikei Horav   *3417 Knox Place*   (O)

Community Center of Israel   *2440 Esplanade*   *882-2400*   (C)

Concourse Center of Israel   *2510 Valentine Avenue*   *295-7700* (O)

Congregation Anshe Emes   *713 East 222nd Street*   *231-5036* (O)

Congregation Beth Jacob   *1461 Leland Avenue*   *892-1339*   (O)

Congregation Hope of Israel   *843 Walton Avenue*   *292-6637*   (O)

Congregation Joseph Ben Meyer   *80 West Kingsbridge Road* (O)

Congregation Kehal Adath Jeshurun   *2222 Cruger Avenue*   *653-4698* (O)

Congregation Lanzuter Beth David   *2364 Woodhull Avenue*   (O)

Congregation Linas Hazedek   *1115 Ward Avenue*   (O)

Congregation Lubavitch of the Bronx   *3414 Olinville Avenue*   (O)

Congregation Mercaz Horav   *2832 Valentine Avenue*   (O)

Congregation of Edenwald   *1014 East 227th Street*   *881-4921* (O)

Congregation Ohel Moshe   *2149 Wallace Avenue*   *792-8544* (O)

Congregation Ohel Moshe Bnai Joseph   *2144 Muliner Avenue* (O)

Congregation Shaaray Tefila   *1744 Eastburn Avenue*   (O)

Congregation Sons of Israel   *2521 Cruger Avenue*   *231-6213* (O)

Congregation Toras Chaim of Co-op City   *620 Baychester Avenue* (O)
671-0310

Congregation Torei Zohov   *2341 Wallace Avenue*   (O)

Conservative Synagogue Adath Israel of Riverdale   *West 250th Street &*
Henry Hudson Parkway East   *543-8400*   (C)

Co-op City Jewish Center   *900 Co-op City Boulevard*   *671-4579* (C)

Educational Jewish Center   *805 Astor Avenue*   *OL5-9865*   (O)

First Van Nest Hebrew Congregation   *1712 Garfield Street* (O)

Ghetto Lodz Memorial Synagogue   *2435 Kingsland Avenue* (O)

Gun Hill Jewish Center   *3380 Reservoir Oval East*   *652-6700* (O)

Hebrew Center of East Bronx   *1276 Commonwealth Avenue*   (O)
829-1772

Hebrew Institute of Riverdale   *3700 Henry Hudson Parkway East* (O)
794-4730

Hebrew Tabernacle of Pelham Parkway   *2150 Holland Avenue*   (O)
822-8756

Intervale Jewish Center   *1024 Intervale Avenue*   (C)

Jewish Center of Highbridge   *1178 Nelson Avenue*   *293-0713*   (O)

Jewish Center of Pelham Bay   *1807 Mahan Avenue*   *892-8171*   (O)

Jewish Center of Unionport   *2137 Ellis Avenue*   *TA2-8601*   (O)

Jewish Center of Violet Park   *3350 Seymor Avenue*   *655-8693*   (O)

Jewish Center of Wakefield & Edenwald   *641 East 233rd Street*   (O)
655-8693

Kingsbridge Center of Israel   *3115 Corlear Avenue*   *548-1678*   (O)

Kingsbridge Heights Jewish Center   *124 Eams Place*   *549-4120*   (O)

Morris Park Hebrew Center   *1812 Paulding Avenue*   *822-8669* (O)

Moshulu Jewish Center   *3044 Hull Avenue*   *547-1515*   (O)

Nathan Strauss Jewish Center   *3512 DeKalb Avenue*   *KI7-1616*   (O)

Ohel Torah Synagogue   *629 West 239th Street*   *543-5618*   (O)

Pelham Parkway Jewish Center   *900 Pelham Parkway South*   (C)
792-6450

Riverdale Jewish Center   *3700 Independence Avenue*   *548-1850*   (O)

Riverdale Temple   *West 246th Street & Independence Avenue* (R)
548-3800

Roosevelt Synagogue   *2060 Wallace Avenue*   *UN3-5200*   (O)

Jacob Schiff Hebrew Center   *2510 Valentine Avenue*   *295-2510*   (C)

Sephardic Shaare Rachamim of East Bronx   *100 Co-op City Blvd.* (O)
671-8882

Nathan Strauss Jewish Center   *3512 DeKalb Avenue*   *KI7-1616* (O)

Temple Beth El of City Island   *480 City Island Avenue*   *885-9865*   (R)

Temple Beth El of Co-op City   *920 Baychester Avenue*   *671-9719* (R)

Temple Emanu-El   *2000 Benedict Avenue*   *822-9337*   (C)

Temple Judea   *615 Reiss Place*   *881-5118* (R)
Throggs Neck Jewish Center   *2918 Lafayette Avenue*   *822-9829* (C)
Van Cortlandt Jewish Center   *3880 Sedgwick Avenue*   *884-6105* (O)
Young Israel of Astor Gardens   *1328 Allerton Avenue*   *653-1363* (O)
Young Israel of Co-op City   *147-1 Dreiser Loop*   *671-2300* (O)
Young Israel of Kingsbridge   *2620 University Avenue*   *298-3910* (O)
Young Israel of Moshulu Parkway   *100 East 208th Street*   *882-8181* (O)
Young Israel of Parkchester   *1375 Virginia Avenue*   *822-9576* (O)

Young Israel of Pelham Parkway   *Barns & Lydig Avenues*   *824-0630*(O)
Young Israel of Riverdale   *4502 Henry Hudson Parkway East*   (O)
548-4765

MIKVEHS

Etz Chaim Mikveh   *708 Mace Avenue*   *798-6173*
Riverdale Mikveh   *3710 Henry Hudson Parkway*   *796-4730*

Staten Island

Staten Island's one Jewish community center serves the needs of its Jewish population of 32,000. Geography and limited transportation facilities have kept Staten Island and its Jewish community small. The opening of the Verrazano Narrows Bridge in 1965, connecting Brooklyn to Staten Island, brought a building boom to Staten Island. Instant Jewish communities, such as Willowbrook, were created.

Driving Tour #12
STATEN ISLAND

New York City's biggest bargain is still the Staten Island ferry. The 20-minute ferry-ride passes the Statue of Liberty, Ellis Island, and offers a spectacular view of the Wall Street skyscrapers, including the World Trade Towers.

Take Staten Island Ferry at Battery Park (Lower Manhattan) to St. George, Staten Island. Drive from ferry terminal southward along Bay Street to Water Street (Stapleton). Turn right on Water Street (opposite park) and drive two small blocks to Wright Street. Turn right at Wright Street.

1. Ferry Terminal
   (Tompkinsville/St. George)
2. Port Richmond
3. Willowbrook

STATEN ISLAND

Stop 1. CONGREGATION TIFERETH ISRAEL (*orig.) Wright Street

The first Jewish settlements in Staten Island were near the ferry terminal. Congregation Tifereth Israel was organized in 1916 in Stapleton, as the Hebrew Alliance, renaming itself in 1927, when the synagogue was erected. In 1977, as the neighborhood deteriorated, the congregation sold the building to a local church and merged with Congregation B'nai Jeshurun of Staten Island.

Turn right at Van Duzer Street and continue on Van Duzer Street to Victory Boulevard. Turn left onto Victory Boulevard.

Stop 2. NEW BRIGHTON JEWISH CONGREGATION (originally CONGREGATION B'NAI JESHURUN OF STATEN ISLAND) 199 Victory Boulevard

Staten Island has had a Jewish community since the 1850s. The first congregation, B'nai Jeshurun of Staten Island, was organized in 1887. Its three-story frame synagogue was built in 1891. The congregation remained in the building until 1971, when it was sold to a funeral parlor and then to a nursery school, and moved to its present site in Westerleigh. In 1978, plans were made to restore the original building as a functioning synagogue and to have it listed as an official New York City landmark.

Continue along Victory Boulevard for one block. At Jersey Street turn right.

Stop 3. CONGREGATION AGUDATH ACHIM ANSHE CHESED (orig.)   386 Jersey Street

In 1900, the expanding community, feeling the need for a second congregation, incorporated Agudath Achim at New Brighton. In 1970 the changing neighborhood forced the congregation to move and its building was sold to a local church.

Continue along Jersey Street to Prospect Avenue. Turn left on Prospect Avenue and drive to Clinton Avenue. Continue on Clinton Avenue and turn left at Henderson Avenue.

---

*The author uses the abbreviation "orig." to designate that the named institution is no longer functioning.

Exterior view of Congregation B'nai Jeshurun of Staten Island, Staten Island's first synagogue.

Stop 4. SAILOR'S SNUG HARBOR PARK   Henderson Avenue

The Harbor was founded by Robert Richard Randall as a home for "aged, decrepid, and worn-out sailors." The Harbor's trustees moved the institution to a new site on the North Carolina coast. Temple Israel, Staten Island's only Reform congregation, was organized in 1948. Its initial services were held in the Sailor's Snug Harbor.

Continue on Henderson Avenue and turn left at Kissel Avenue. Drive along Kissel Avenue and turn left onto Castleton Avenue. Drive three blocks along Castleton Avenue and turn right at Hart Boulevard. Continue to Forest Avenue and turn right.

Stop 5. TEMPLE ISRAEL REFORM CONGREGATION
315 Forest Avenue

Organized in 1948, Temple Israel's initial services were held in the Sailor's Snug Harbor. After their second home, the Gans mansion, was destroyed by fire, the present building was erected. It was designed in 1964 by Percival Goodman, who designed over fifty synagogues throughout the United States. The synagogue has a flexible floor plan on the sanctuary level and classroom and meeting facilities on its lower level.

Drive west along Forest Avenue. Turn right at Elizabeth Street and continue for two blocks to Delafield Avenue. Turn left on Delafield Avenue.

159

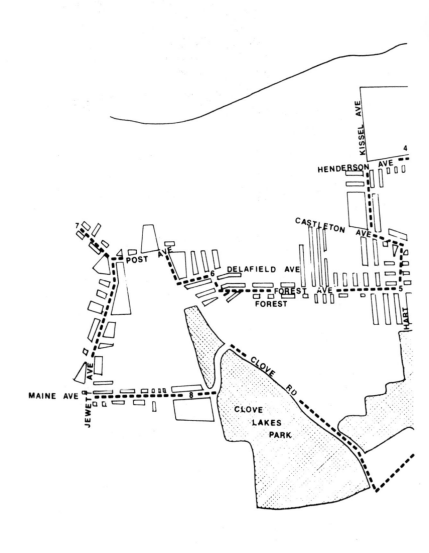

DRIVING TOUR #12: STATEN ISLAND

STATEN ISLAND SYNAGOGUES

Arden Heights Boulevard Jewish Center   *1766 Arthur Kill Road*   (C)
948-6782

Congregation Agudas Achim Anshe Chesed   *641 Delafield Avenue*   (O)
442-9445

Congregation Agudath Shomrei Hadas   *98 Rupert Avenue*   *761-9578*   (O

Congregation Ahavath Israel   *7630 Amboy Road*   *356-8740*   (C)

Congregation Ahavath Sholom   *2044 Richmond Avenue*   *761-8446* (C)

Congregation Beth Shloime of Staten Island   *84 Oakland Street* (O)
761-5559

Congregation Beth Yehuda   *239 Crafton Avenue*   *698-8830* (O)

Congregation Bnai Israel   *45 Twombly Avenue*   *987-8188* (C)

Congregation Bnai Jeshurun   *275 Martling Avenue*   *981-5550*   (C)

Congregation Bnai Zion   *4150 Amboy Road*   *984-8660* (O)

Congregation Hayosher V'Hatov   *61 Rupert Avenue*   *698-2585*   (O)

Temple Beth Abraham   *1278 Rockland Avenue*   *698-2978* (R)

Temple Emanu-El   *984 Post Avenue*   *442-9488*   (C)

Temple Israel Reform Congregation   *315 Forest Avenue*   *727-2231* (R)

Young Israel of Eltingville   *374 Ridgewood Avenue*   *984-8393*

Young Israel of Staten Island   *835 Forest Hill Road*   *761-9578*

MIKVEHS

Mikveh Israel   *61 Rupert Avenue*   *698-4066*

Young Israel of Staten Island Mikveh   *835 Forest Hill Road*   *761-9578*

163

Jewish Entertainment

CAFES AND NIGHTCLUBS

NOTE: Some of these cafes and nightclubs do not serve kosher foods. It is recommended to ask whether or not kosher food is served.

The following cafes and nightclubs offer supper and drinks followed by a floorshow featuring Israeli, Yiddish, and Greek entertainment (music and dancing).

Baba Cafe   *91-33 63rd Drive*   *Rego Park, Queens*   *275-2660*

Feenjon Cafe   *117 MacDougal Street, Manhattan*   *254-3630*

Jerusalem II   *1375 Broadway*   *Manhattan*

JEWISH MUSEUMS
AND ART GALLERIES

Abraham Goodman House   *129 West 67th Street, Manhattan*
   362-8060.

Board of Jewish Education   *425 West 58th Street, Manhattan*
   245-8200. Open Monday-Thursday 12 noon-5 P.M.

Chassidic Art Institute   *375 Kingston Avenue, Brooklyn 774-9149. Open*
   Monday-Thursday 12 noon-5 P.M., Sunday 11 A.M.-6 P.M.

Educational Alliance   *197 East Broadway, Manhattan   475-6200. Open*
   Sunday-Thursday 10 A.M.-10 P.M.

International Synagogue   *Kennedy International Airport (Chapel exit),*
   Queens   656-5044. Open Monday-Friday 10 A.M.-4 P.M.

The Jewish Museum   *Fifth Avenue & East 92nd Street, Manhattan*
   860-1888. Open Monday-Thursday 12 noon-5 P.M., Sunday 11 A.M.-6
   P.M.

Leo Baeck Institute   *129 East 73rd Street, Manhattan   744-6400. Open*
   Monday-Friday 9 A.M.-5 P.M.

Mid-Town YMHA   *344 East 14th Street, Manhattan   674-7200. Open*
   Sunday-Thursday 12 noon-8 P.M., Friday 10 A.M.-2 P.M.

92nd Street YMHA   *Lexington Avenue & East 92nd Street, Manhattan*
   427-6000. Open Sunday-Friday 9 A.M.-10 P.M.

Union of American Hebrew Congregations   *838 Fifth Avenue, Manhattan*
   249-0100. Open Monday-Friday 9:30 A.M.-4:30 P.M.

Yeshiva University Museum   *2520 Amsterdam Avenue, Manhattan*
   960-5390. Open Tuesday-Thursday 11 A.M.-5 P.M., Sunday 11 A.M.-6
   P.M.

Yivo Institute for Jewish Research   *1048 Fifth Avenue, Manhattan*
   535-6700. Open Monday-Friday 9:30 A.M.-5:30 P.M.

ISRAELI FOLK DANCING

East Meadow   Eisenhower Park Roller Rink - Field #4
(718) 275-0265
Tuesday 7:30 - 10:00 p.m. (July - Aug.)   *Honey Goldfein-Perry*
New York City   Congregation Shaare Zedek   *212 West 93rd
Street* (718) 699-1248
Sunday 7:00 - 11:00 p.m. *Naftaly Kadosh*
Columbia University (Earl Hall)   *Broadway & West
117th Street*
Monday 7:15 - 10:15 p.m. *Ruth Goodman Burger*
(212) 280-511, 888-1770
92nd Street YMHA   *1395 Lexington Avenue*   *(2nd floor)*
(212) 888-1770
Wednesday 8:00 - 11:00 p.m. *Ruth Goodman Burger/
Danny Uziel*
Ethnic Arts Center   *179 Varick Street (201) 836-2655*
Thursday 8:00 - 11:00 p.m. *Tamar Yablonski*

(Brooklyn)   J.C.H. 7802 Bay Parkway (718) 331-6800
Tuesday 8:00 - 11:00 p.m. Rene Diamond

(Queens)   Central Queens YMHA 67-09 108th Street
(718) 888-1770
Tuesday 8:00 - 11:00 p.m. *Honey Goldfein-Perry*
Flushing YMHA   *45-35 Kissena Boulevard (718) 461-3030*
Call for schedule.

Tenafly   JCC on the Palisades   *411 East Clinton Avenue
(201) 569-7900 or (201) 836-2655*
Sunday & Tuesday 7:30 - 10:30 p.m. Tamar Yablonski

YIDDISH THEATER

American Jewish Theatre   *1395 Lexington Avenue (92nd St. YMHA),*
    Manhattan   427-4410

Educational Alliance   *197 East Broadway, Manhattan   724-9957*

Folksbeine Playhouse   *123 East 55th Street (Central Synagogue),*
    Manhattan   755-2231

Jewish Repertory Theatre   *344 East 14th Street (Mid-Town YMHA),*
    Manhattan   674-7200

Norman Thomas Theatre   *East 33rd Street & Park Avenue, Manhattan*

Town Hall   *123 West 43rd Street, Manhattan   840-2824*

BOAT TOUR
of
JEWISH NEW YORK

*Join Oscar Israelowitz, author of "Guide to Jewish N.Y.C.,"
on a fun-filled 3-hour boat tour around Jewish New York. See
such thrilling sites as the Statue of Liberty, Ellis Island, First
Jewish Settlement in New Amsterdam (1654), Castle Garden,
Holocaust Memorial Museum, Lower East Side, Williamsburg,
Jewish Harlem, Yeshiva University, Jewish Theological Seminary, and much more.*

For tickets, reservations, and further information
about this special boat tour and walking tours of the
Lower East Side, please call or write to:

Mr. Oscar Israelowitz
P.O. Box 228
Brooklyn, New York 11229

(718) 951 - 7072

GUIDED TOURS
OF THE
LOWER EAST SIDE

- Visit the "old neighborhood"..
- Explore Orchard Street...
- See historic synagogues...
- Enjoy wine-tasting in a kosher wine cellar...

FOR FURTHER INFORMATION &
RESERVATIONS CALL
(718) 951-7072
Oscar Israelowitz

Glossary

Ashkenazic *Pertaining to Jews who lived originally in the Rhineland and spread through central Europe; the term eventually was used to include all Jews who observe the "German" synagogue ritual. The common language spoken by Ashkenaz Jews is Yiddish.*

beth (bais) hamedrash *Place where rabbinical literature is studied; meeting-place of a study group; the small sanctuary of a large synagogue usually used for daily prayer service.*

bimah (tayvah) *The platform from which the Torah is read to the congregation during prayer services in the synagogue.*

Chassid *A member of a Jewish mystical sect founded in Eastern Europe in the 18th century.*

chulent *A special stew prepared for the Sabbath meal.*

kiddush *Special prayer recited over wine before the Sabbath meal.*

kosher (kashruth) *Ritually fit for use. (Correct or proper)*

lulav *Palm branch used at prayer services during the holiday of Succos.*

maariv *Evening prayer.*

matzoh *Unleavened bread eaten during the holiday of Passover.*

mikveh *Ritual bath; ritualarium.*

mincha *Afternoon prayer.*

minyan   *According to the Orthodox tradition, ten males over the age of thirteen, the minimum attendance required for congregational worship.*

Rosh Hashana   *Jewish New Year.*

Sephardic   *Pertaining to the occidental branch of European Jews settling in Spain and Portugal.*

shmahtes   *Yiddish term for rags.*

shmooz   *Yiddish term for conversation.*

shmura (matzoh)   *Hebrew term for guarded or closely inspected.*

shteebl   *Yiddish term for small room used for prayer services.*

shul   *Yiddish term for synagogue.*

Simchas Torah   *Jewish holiday following Succos celebrating the "rejoicing with the Torah."*

Succos   *Jewish holiday following Yom Kippur (Day of Atonement) celebrating the journey of Israel through the desert after the exodus from Egypt. As their ancestors dwelt in temporary booths or shelters (Succah, in Hebrew), so do contemporary Jews live in Succos during this week-long holiday.*

tashlich   *Prayer recited on Rosh Hashana (Jewish New Year) when the Jews symbolically "cast away" their sins into the waters.*

yeshiva   *Hebrew (day) school.*

Yiddish   *A high German language spoken by Jews chiefly in Eastern Europe and areas to which Jews from Eastern Europe have migrated. It is commonly written in Hebrew characters.*

Bibliography

Abelow, S.P. *History of Brooklyn Jewry.* New York: Sheba Publishing, 1937.

Anderson, G. A New-Fashioned Schoolhouse. *Architectural Record,* October 1981.

Brooklyn Daily Eagle Almanac. New York: Brooklyn Daily Eagle, 1889-1929.

de Breffny, B. *The Synagogue.* New York: Macmillan Publishing Co., 1978.

Encyclopedia Judaica. Jerusalem, Israel: Keter Publishing House, Jerusalem Ltd., 1972.

Grafton, J. *New York in the Nineteenth Century.* New York: Dover Publications, 1977.

Gurock, J. *When Harlem Was Jewish.* New York: Columbia University Press, 1979.

Howe, I. & Libo, K. *How We Lived.* New York: Plume Books, 1979.

Israelowitz, O. *Synagogues of New York City.* New York: Dover Publications, 1982.

Landesman, A.F. *Brownsville.* New York: Block Publishers, 1969.

Postal, B. & Koppman, L. *Jewish Landmarks of New York.* New York: Fleet Press, 1978.

Recent American Synagogue Architecture-Catalogue. The Jewish Museum of New York, 1963.

Sanders, R. & Gillon, E. *The Lower East Side.* New York: Dover Publications, 1979.

The Universal Jewish Encyclopedia, New York: The Universal Jewish Encyclopedia Company, Inc. 1948.

Two Hundred Years of American Synagogue Architecture-Catalogue. Waltham, MA: American Jewish Historical Society, 1976.

White, N. & Willensky, E. *A.I.A. Guide to New York City.* New York: Collier Books, 1978.

Younger, W.L. *Old Brooklyn.* New York: Dover Publications, 1978.

Guide to Jewish Europe

Western Europe Edition

This guide is a "must" for the Jewish traveler to Europe with do-it-yourself tours of London, Venice, Paris, Rome, and Amsterdam. There is information on kosher restaurants and hotels, synagogues and mikvehs, Jewish landmarks and museums, youth hostels, and railroad and Sabbath candlelighting timetables.

Paperback 232 pages $11.50

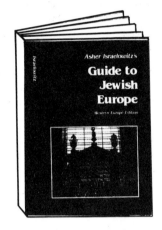

Guide to Jewish U.S.A.

Volume I
The Northeast

The most comprehensive historic and travel guide on Jewish travel in the United States contains information on Jewish historic landmarks, Jewish museums, kosher restaurants, synagogues, mikvehs, and over 100 illustrations.

Paperback 320 pages $11.50

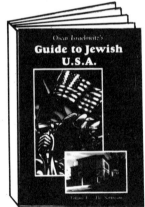

Synagogues of New York City

This pictorial survey of the great synagogues in all five boroughs of New York City contains 123 black and white and color photographs. These photographs outline the history of the Jewish presence in New York City and the role synagogues played in sustaining it. The high quality book makes a fine gift for the Judaica collector.

Paperback 86 pages $7.50

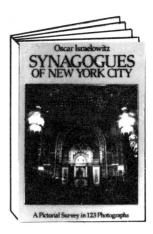

The Lower East Side Guide

This unique guide is designed for the tourist and contains a complete-do-it-yourself walking tour of this historic Jewish neighborhood. It is also designed for the shopper and contains a shopping directory with information on where to find the bargains!

Paperback 124 pages $6.00

Synagogues of the World Photographs

For the collector of exquisite color photographs from the private collection of Oscar Israelowitz. The 15 ready-to-frame prints (10" x 6") includes interior and exterior views of such great synagogues in Florence, Amsterdam, London, Gibraltar, Glasgow, Jerusalem, and Curaçao.

$5.00

Guide to Jewish New York City
1983 Edition

The original 1983 edition contains 10 complete do-it-yourself tours of the largest Jewish city in the world. There are Jewish historic landmarks, Jewish museums, synagogues, kosher restaurants, Israeli folk dancing, and Yiddish theatres.

Paperback 152 pages $3.50

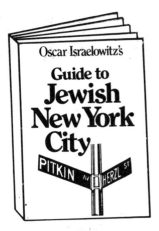

Guide to Jewish New York City
Revised Edition

The expanded and updated edition contains 12 complete do-it-yourself tours with information on Chassidic neighborhoods, the Lower East Side, historic landmark synagogues, mikvehs, and Jewish entertainment.

Paperback 200 pages $8.50

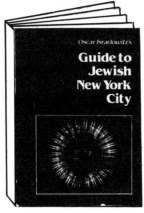

Shopper's Guide to Borough Park

A unique guide of this Chassidic section of Brooklyn, New York, known as the "Jerusalem of America." Complete with vintage photographs, a do-it-yourself walking tour, and, of course, the shopping.

Paperback 60 pages $3.00

BIOGRAPHICAL SKETCH

Born in Brussels, Belgium, Mr. Oscar Israelowitz brings a rich background to his mission of documenting Jewish neighborhoods. He is a professional architect and photographer. Among his noted architectural projects are the Synagogue and Holocaust Center of the Bobover Chassidim in Borough Park and the Yeshiva Rabbi Chaim Berlin (elementary school) in the Flatbush section of Brooklyn. He has also designed several homes and villas in the United States, Haiti, and Israel. He has exhibited his photographs in museums throughout the New York area, including the Brooklyn and Whitney Museums. Mr. Israelowitz has appeared on several television and radio programs including NBC's *First Estate - Religion In Review.* Mr. Israelowitz gives lectures on various Jewish travel topics and has now expanded his walking and bus tours of Jewish neighborhoods to Jewish boat tours around Manhattan and a series of Jewish Heritage Tours of the Caribbean and Eastern and Western Europe.

Index

NOTES

NOTES

NOTES

NOTES

NOTES

NOTES

NOTES

NOTES

NOTES

NOTES

NOTES

NOTES